Who Are You?

TEST YOUR EMOTIONAL
INTELLIGENCE

Who Are You?

TEST YOUR EMOTIONAL INTELLIGENCE

50 Easy-to-Score Quizzes

THOMAS J. CRAUGHWELL

BLACK DOG
& LEVENTHAL
PUBLISHERS
NEW YORK

Published by
Black Dog & Leventhal Publishers, Inc.
151 West 19th Street New York, NY 10011

Distributed by
Workman Publishing Company
225 Varick Street New York, NY 10014

Manufactured in China
Cover and interior design by Liz Dreisbach

ISBN-13: 978-1-57912-904-0
h g f e d c b a
Library of Congress Cataloging-in-Publication Data available upon request

CONTENTS

INTRODUCTION

What is emotional intelligence, also known as EQ? It is a bit like common sense—it is a skill, an innate, very perceptive way of looking at yourself and at other people. It doesn't matter how much education you have, or how varied and rich your life and work experiences may have been, or how high your IQ score is—none of these things will predict if you have been blessed with emotional intelligence.

You can see living, breathing examples of this every day. Brilliant, successful individuals have no people skills, while an individual with fewer advantages seems to get along well with everyone. And the thing the Ivy League university president lacks but the neighborhood handyman possesses is more than charm or charisma.

According to psychologists Dr. Travis Bradberry and Dr. Jean Greaves, authors of The Emotional Intelligence Quick Book, emotional intelligence is a combination of skills. Self-awareness and self-management are characteristic traits of the person who possesses EQ. Then there are social awareness and relationship management, which relate to how the person with EQ interacts with other people. Of course, some people by nature are more emotionally intelligent than others. Nonetheless, you can become more emotionally intelligent by paying attention to your emotions and behavior and managing them, while also understanding what motivates other people and working at improving your relationships with others.

Each EQ test comes with a scoring system that will help you to gauge your emotional intelligence. Based on the scores in the individual tests, you will be able to judge if your EQ needs some work.

As you work to boost your emotional intelligence, some discomfort will probably be involved. You will have to take a long, candid look at yourself and assess your own positive and negative qualities, then set out to improve yourself. Along the way there are all the other people you will encounter. Not all of them will be pleasant. A nineteenth-century Italian saint, John Bosco, once said that the most difficult penance is putting up with tiresome people. Yet the only way to become more emotionally intelligent is to make that open and honest assessment of yourself, while practicing how to get along with just about everyone else.

The fifty quizzes included in this small book are designed to make you more aware of yourself and your relationships with others—in the family, in the workplace, in friendships, and in romantic relationships. Answer the questions honestly and you will be surprised by what you can learn about your own level of emotional intelligence. And if your score in some of the tests isn't as high as you'd like, then you will know what facets of your EQ need work.

Have fun getting emotionally smarter!

CHAPTER 1

ON THE JOB

Every morning, when you walk into your workplace, you are walking into an emotional mine field. And it's not just your boss and co-workers you have to keep an eye on, it's also clients, vendors, service staff, even the cashier in the cafeteria. All of them come to work every day with their issues, worries, ambitions, aggravations, and resentments. And so do you. We are still a long way from replacing the human work force with robots, so as long as you work with people, you also have to deal with their emotions, and, for that matter, you have to deal with your emotions, too.

You've probably encountered the co-worker who keeps his or her emotions bottled up. In moments of success, he or she is cool and aloof. In moments of crisis, he or she is detached. Such people can be very rigid about process and procedures, which makes them difficult to work with. Furthermore, workers of this type tend to give off an unfriendly vibe: you probably won't see them playing softball at the company summer picnic or singing carols at the holiday party.

At the other end of the spectrum is the co-worker who never has an unexpressed emotion. Joy, frustration, success, or despair—he or she lets it all out. It can be exhausting for such a person's co-workers (not to mention noisy).

In 2002, Wendy Alfus Rothman, a member of The Employment Roundtable, wrote a short piece entitled "Developing Emotional Intelligence in the Workplace." In her essay, Rothman said, "Developing emotional intelligence in the workplace means acknowledging that emotions are always present, and doing something intelligent with them."

In the quizzes that follow, you'll be presented with questions and scenarios intended to help you handle your own emotions on the job, while staying attuned to the emotions of the people around you.

An emotionally intelligent employee or manager does a good job even in a stressful situation; works well as part of a team; motivates, perhaps even inspires others; and maintains cordial, productive relationships with co-workers and superiors. That sounds like a tall order, but the cornerstone of emotional intelligence is keeping the most violent emotions in check, learning to be empathetic, and responding appropriately to a variety of unexpected situations in the workplace.

The "On the Job" quizzes are designed to help you understand and work with even difficult people, while also helping you become a better employee or manager.

✐ How Well Do You Cooperate with Others?

1 I like things done in a certain way, so it is difficult for me to work with others.

Completely true　　*Somewhat true/false*　　*Completely false*

Mostly true　　*Mostly false*

2 I become angry if someone else is the center of attention.

Completely true　　*Somewhat true/false*　　*Completely false*

Mostly true　　*Mostly false*

3 I must follow the same routine every day.

Completely true　　*Somewhat true/false*　　*Completely false*

Mostly true　　*Mostly false*

4 If people offend me, I snub them.

Completely true　　*Somewhat true/false*　　*Completely false*

Mostly true　　*Mostly false*

5 Lack of structure upsets me.

Completely true　　*Somewhat true/false*　　*Completely false*

Mostly true　　*Mostly false*

6 I am most comfortable when I am in charge.

Completely true　　*Somewhat true/false*　　*Completely false*

Mostly true　　*Mostly false*

7 I often worry that I am being taken advantage of.

Completely true　　*Somewhat true/false*　　*Completely false*

Mostly true　　*Mostly false*

8 I do my best work when I work on my own.

Completely true   *Somewhat true/false*   *Completely false*

   Mostly true   *Mostly false*

9 I can be intimidating.

Completely true   *Somewhat true/false*   *Completely false*

   Mostly true   *Mostly false*

10 Most people do not meet my standards.

Completely true   *Somewhat true/false*   *Completely false*

   Mostly true   *Mostly false*

SCORING ·

Each answer is awarded a specific number of points.

Completely true: *1 point*
Mostly true: *2 points*
Somewhat true/false: *3 points*
Mostly false: *4 points*
Completely false: *5 points*

50–40: You work well with others.
39–30: You're basically a team player.
Below 30: You'll never be first pick at the office softball game.

✏️ How Responsible Are You?

1 I am rarely late for an appointment.

Completely true　　　*Somewhat true/false*　　　*Completely false*

　　　　Mostly true　　　　　*Mostly false*

2 I am not afraid of responsibility.

Completely true　　　*Somewhat true/false*　　　*Completely false*

　　　　Mostly true　　　　　*Mostly false*

3 I prefer a busy, fast-paced job.

Completely true　　　*Somewhat true/false*　　　*Completely false*

　　　　Mostly true　　　　　*Mostly false*

4 I like to be productive all day.

Completely true　　　*Somewhat true/false*　　　*Completely false*

　　　　Mostly true　　　　　*Mostly false*

5 At work, I follow up on all my assignments to monitor how they are progressing.

Completely true　　　*Somewhat true/false*　　　*Completely false*

　　　　Mostly true　　　　　*Mostly false*

6 I enjoy working with my hands.

Completely true　　　*Somewhat true/false*　　　*Completely false*

　　　　Mostly true　　　　　*Mostly false*

7 I do my best to meet deadlines.

Completely true　　　*Somewhat true/false*　　　*Completely false*

　　　　Mostly true　　　　　*Mostly false*

8 I have good control over my impulses.

Completely true   *Somewhat true/false*   *Completely false*

Mostly true   *Mostly false*

9 My work habits are fairly consistent.

Completely true   *Somewhat true/false*   *Completely false*

Mostly true   *Mostly false*

10 I enjoy problem-solving.

Completely true   *Somewhat true/false*   *Completely false*

Mostly true   *Mostly false*

SCORING ································

Each answer is awarded a specific number of points.

Completely true: *5 points*
Mostly true: *4 points*
Somewhat true/false: *3 points*
Mostly false: *2 points*
Completely false: *1 point*

50–40: You're a responsible, trustworthy individual.
39–30: You're a fairly responsible person.
Below 30: You're not the best choice for an important assignment or a tight deadline.

✏️ How Do You Function at Work?

1 Even in a crisis, I stay composed and clearheaded.

Completely true   *Somewhat true/false*   *Completely false*

Mostly true   *Mostly false*

2 Deadlines do not freak me out.

Completely true   *Somewhat true/false*   *Completely false*

Mostly true   *Mostly false*

3 If I make a mistake, I admit it.

Completely true   *Somewhat true/false*   *Completely false*

Mostly true   *Mostly false*

4 I make a sincere effort to meet my commitments.

Completely true   *Somewhat true/false*   *Completely false*

Mostly true   *Mostly false*

5 I believe that staying organized is the key to good job performance.

Completely true   *Somewhat true/false*   *Completely false*

Mostly true   *Mostly false*

6 I welcome new ideas and new ways of doing things.

Completely true   *Somewhat true/false*   *Completely false*

Mostly true   *Mostly false*

7 I can juggle more than one assignment at a time.

Completely true   *Somewhat true/false*   *Completely false*

Mostly true   *Mostly false*

8 If the requirements of a project change, I can adapt.

Completely true   *Somewhat true/false*   *Completely false*

Mostly true   *Mostly false*

9 To achieve my goals, I'm not afraid to take calculated risks.

Completely true   *Somewhat true/false*   *Completely false*

Mostly true   *Mostly false*

10 I am interested in new methods and new technologies that will improve my job performance.

Completely true   *Somewhat true/false*   *Completely false*

Mostly true   *Mostly false*

SCORING ································

Each answer is awarded a specific number of points.

Completely true: *5 points*
Mostly true: *4 points*
Somewhat true/false: *3 points*
Mostly false: *2 points*
Completely false: *1 point*

50–40: You're a valuable, reliable employee.
39–30: You have something to contribute in the workplace.
Below 30: You're not functioning at an especially high level on the job.

✏️ How Confident Are You?

1 I would never sing a solo at a party.

Completely true　　　*Somewhat true/false*　　　*Completely false*

　　　　Mostly true　　　　　　*Mostly false*

2 Before I leave the house, I check myself in the mirror.

Completely true　　　*Somewhat true/false*　　　*Completely false*

　　　　Mostly true　　　　　　*Mostly false*

3 I would never be part of the studio audience on a game show—I'm afraid I'd get called up onstage.

Completely true　　　*Somewhat true/false*　　　*Completely false*

　　　　Mostly true　　　　　　*Mostly false*

4 If someone does or says something foolish, I feel very uncomfortable.

Completely true　　　*Somewhat true/false*　　　*Completely false*

　　　　Mostly true　　　　　　*Mostly false*

5 I make mistakes if someone watches me work.

Completely true　　　*Somewhat true/false*　　　*Completely false*

　　　　Mostly true　　　　　　*Mostly false*

6 I don't feel comfortable wearing bright colors or stylish clothes.

Completely true　　　*Somewhat true/false*　　　*Completely false*

　　　　Mostly true　　　　　　*Mostly false*

7 I am never at ease undressing in a locker room or walking around in my bathing suit at the beach.

Completely true   *Somewhat true/false*   *Completely false*

Mostly true   *Mostly false*

8 At office meetings, I rarely offer a suggestion.

Completely true   *Somewhat true/false*   *Completely false*

Mostly true   *Mostly false*

9 When dealing with rude people, it is easier for me to walk away silently than to confront them.

Completely true   *Somewhat true/false*   *Completely false*

Mostly true   *Mostly false*

10 I have trouble standing up for myself.

Completely true   *Somewhat true/false*   *Completely false*

Mostly true   *Mostly false*

SCORING

Each answer is awarded a specific number of points.

Completely true: *1 point*
Mostly true: *2 points*
Somewhat true/false: *3 points*
Mostly false: *4 points*
Completely false: *5 points*

50–40: You're a self-assured person.
39–30: You're more or less confident.
Below 30: A little assertiveness training wouldn't hurt.

✏ What Type of Employee Are You?

1 I think of myself as a team player.

Completely true   *Somewhat true/false*   *Completely false*

Mostly true   *Mostly false*

2 I like having clearly defined goals.

Completely true   *Somewhat true/false*   *Completely false*

Mostly true   *Mostly false*

3 I feel a sense of accomplishment when my peers praise my problem-solving skills.

Completely true   *Somewhat true/false*   *Completely false*

Mostly true   *Mostly false*

4 The thing I dislike most in the workplace is incompetence.

Completely true   *Somewhat true/false*   *Completely false*

Mostly true   *Mostly false*

5 In my ideal career, I'd keep learning new skills.

Completely true   *Somewhat true/false*   *Completely false*

Mostly true   *Mostly false*

6 When I'm interacting with coworkers, the best approach for me is to be impartial and professional.

Completely true   *Somewhat true/false*   *Completely false*

Mostly true   *Mostly false*

7 When I'm doing problem-solving, what I value most is finding new ways to prevent the problem from recurring.

Completely true   *Somewhat true/false*   *Completely false*

      Mostly true   *Mostly false*

8 When I'm making a decision, I make a logical assessment of all the facts.

Completely true   *Somewhat true/false*   *Completely false*

      Mostly true   *Mostly false*

9 The best reward my employer could give me would be more managerial authority.

Completely true   *Somewhat true/false*   *Completely false*

      Mostly true   *Mostly false*

10 Talking with new employees or clients often generates new ideas.

Completely true   *Somewhat true/false*   *Completely false*

      Mostly true   *Mostly false*

SCORING

Each answer is awarded a specific number of points.

Completely true: *1 point*
Mostly true: *2 points*
Somewhat true/false: *3 points*
Mostly false: *4 points*
Completely false: *5 points*

50–40: Call the next job candidate, please.
39–30: You're not ideal on the job, but you're a smart bet.
Below 30: You're the perfect employee.

✏️ What Is Your Personality in the Workplace?

Mark the circle that corresponds to where on the continuum between each of the word/phrase pairs you fall. If you mark 1 or 5, then you identify most strongly with one of the words or phrases in the pair; 2 or 4 less so; 3 you are neutral.

1 methodical ① • ② • ③ • ④ • ⑤ confused

2 communicative ① • ② • ③ • ④ • ⑤ reserved

3 volunteer for assignments ① • ② • ③ • ④ • ⑤ never volunteer for assignments

4 eager for change ① • ② • ③ • ④ • ⑤ like a routine

5 takes direction ① • ② • ③ • ④ • ⑤ hates criticism

6 self-assured ① • ② • ③ • ④ • ⑤ nervous

7 cooperative ① • ② • ③ • ④ • ⑤ resentful

8 prompt ① • ② • ③ • ④ • ⑤ late

9 office door open ① • ② • ③ • ④ • ⑤ office door closed

10 ambitious ① • ② • ③ • ④ • ⑤ apathetic

SCORING ·

50–40: You're the worst job candidate ever.
39–30: You're not even a runner-up.
Below 30: You're a five-star applicant.

How Do You Handle Stress?

1 I have a strong personality.

Completely true   *Somewhat true/false*   *Completely false*

Mostly true   *Mostly false*

2 I suffer from mood swings, more so than most people.

Completely true   *Somewhat true/false*   *Completely false*

Mostly true   *Mostly false*

3 I lash out in stressful situations.

Completely true   *Somewhat true/false*   *Completely false*

Mostly true   *Mostly false*

4 When I feel stressed, I refuse to take on more assignments and responsibilities.

Completely true   *Somewhat true/false*   *Completely false*

Mostly true   *Mostly false*

5 In my circle of friends, I'm known as the perfectionist.

Completely true   *Somewhat true/false*   *Completely false*

Mostly true   *Mostly false*

6 I worry about my health.

Completely true   *Somewhat true/false*   *Completely false*

Mostly true   *Mostly false*

7 I use food or alcohol to help me get through stressful times.

Completely true   *Somewhat true/false*   *Completely false*

Mostly true   *Mostly false*

8 When I'm anxious, I get nauseous.

Completely true   *Somewhat true/false*   *Completely false*

     Mostly true   *Mostly false*

9 Stress makes me physically and emotionally exhausted.

Completely true   *Somewhat true/false*   *Completely false*

     Mostly true   *Mostly false*

10 When I'm under stress, I find it hard to sit still and relax.

Completely true   *Somewhat true/false*   *Completely false*

     Mostly true   *Mostly false*

SCORING ·

Each answer is awarded a specific number of points.

Completely true: *1 point*
Mostly true: *2 points*
Somewhat true/false: *3 points*
Mostly false: *4 points*
Completely false: *5 points*

50–40: You're composed even in stressful situations.
39–30: You handle stress reasonably well.
Below 30: At the first sign of stress, you're ready to crawl under the bed and assume the fetal position.

✎ Do You Have a Persuasive Personality?

1 I try to be courteous to everyone I meet.

Completely true   *Somewhat true/false*   *Completely false*

Mostly true   *Mostly false*

2 Usually, I find it easy to bring people around to my point of view.

Completely true   *Somewhat true/false*   *Completely false*

Mostly true   *Mostly false*

3 Usually, I can talk people into doing what I want them to do.

Completely true   *Somewhat true/false*   *Completely false*

Mostly true   *Mostly false*

4 When making a point, I try to be as clear as possible so everyone will understand what I am trying to explain.

Completely true   *Somewhat true/false*   *Completely false*

Mostly true   *Mostly false*

5 I am rarely nervous when talking to a stranger.

Completely true   *Somewhat true/false*   *Completely false*

Mostly true   *Mostly false*

6 I believe most people think I am friendly.

Completely true   *Somewhat true/false*   *Completely false*

Mostly true   *Mostly false*

7 I think most people enjoy my company.

Completely true   *Somewhat true/false*   *Completely false*

          Mostly true   *Mostly false*

8 I enjoy attending parties and other social functions.

Completely true   *Somewhat true/false*   *Completely false*

          Mostly true   *Mostly false*

9 I have a lot of influence over my family and friends.

Completely true   *Somewhat true/false*   *Completely false*

          Mostly true   *Mostly false*

10 I have always been a good salesperson.

Completely true   *Somewhat true/false*   *Completely false*

          Mostly true   *Mostly false*

SCORING

Each answer is awarded a specific number of points.

Completely true: *5 points*
Mostly true: *4 points*
Somewhat true/false: *3 points*
Mostly false: *2 points*
Completely false: *1 point*

50–40: You have an outgoing, charismatic personality
39–30: You have some persuasive skills.
Below 30: There's no future for you in sales or politics.

CHAPTER 2

YOUR
SOCIAL LIFE

"No man is an island," wrote the 17th-century English poet, John Donne. In other words, we are all part of a community, and the community functions best when its members possess self-awareness.

People who are self-aware have a clear, just understanding of their strengths and weaknesses, their potential, their desires, and how these aspects of their personality can affect other people. We have all had encounters with people who hold long, loud conversations on their cellphone on a train or plane or bus—places where the rest of the passengers can't escape the big-mouthed bore. Anyone with the slightest sense of self-awareness would know to lower his or her voice, or find a more private setting for the phone conversation—the rest room, or perhaps the rear of the vehicle, someplace where he or she will not be disruptive.

Then there are individuals who are slaves to their emotions. Whatever they feel, they express; whether it is the most appropriate time or place to vent their emotions doesn't phase such people. For generations, parents have instructed their children not to discuss religion or politics in public, but the socially clueless go beyond these taboos, droning on and on about their salary, their jobs, their current and past relationships, even the most intimate details of their family life. Nor do such people notice that their insensitive monologue has made just about everyone within earshot feel uncomfortable, even mortified.

Finally, there are the people so caught up in themselves that they cannot empathize with others. Imagine being confined to a hospital bed, and receiving a string of visitors who aren't interested in your condition but only want to talk about their own aches and pains, or their last visit to their doctor, or their most current ailment. Such people are so self-absorbed that even when confronted with a seriously ill friend or relative, they can only think of themselves.

The three types of people we've described are the socially clueless. They have no sense of how they are perceived, or how they have embarrassed or offended the people around them.

The "Your Social Life" quizzes that follow are intended to help you be more aware of what you are doing and saying, control your emotions, and become more empathetic.

✏️ How Social Are You?

1 I have many friends and acquaintances.

Completely true   *Somewhat true/false*   *Completely false*

Mostly true   *Mostly false*

2 In my spare time, I enjoy socializing with family and friends, attending dinner parties, and going to movies.

Completely true   *Somewhat true/false*   *Completely false*

Mostly true   *Mostly false*

3 I am happy to help someone, and I don't expect anything in return.

Completely true   *Somewhat true/false*   *Completely false*

Mostly true   *Mostly false*

4 I am a sympathetic person.

Completely true   *Somewhat true/false*   *Completely false*

Mostly true   *Mostly false*

5 I find it easy to make new friends at a new workplace.

Completely true   *Somewhat true/false*   *Completely false*

Mostly true   *Mostly false*

6 I enjoy interacting with people.

Completely true   *Somewhat true/false*   *Completely false*

Mostly true   *Mostly false*

7 I am moved by stories of people who are sick, suffering, or needy.

Completely true　　*Somewhat true/false*　　*Completely false*

Mostly true　　　　　*Mostly false*

8 I feel at ease in a crowd.

Completely true　　*Somewhat true/false*　　*Completely false*

Mostly true　　　　　*Mostly false*

9 There are times when I am emotional.

Completely true　　*Somewhat true/false*　　*Completely false*

Mostly true　　　　　*Mostly false*

10 I enjoy doing volunteer work.

Completely true　　*Somewhat true/false*　　*Completely false*

Mostly true　　　　　*Mostly false*

SCORING ·

Each answer is awarded a specific number of points.

Completely true: *5 points*
Mostly true: *4 points*
Somewhat true/false: *3 points*
Mostly false: *2 points*
Completely false: *1 point*

50–40: You're a charismatic people person.
39–30: You have average people skills.
Below 30: You don't appear on any party planner's A list.

✏️ What Kind of Friend Are You?

1 If I knew for a fact that a friend's spouse was having an affair, I would say nothing.

Completely true   *Somewhat true/false*   *Completely false*

Mostly true   *Mostly false*

2 If I found that a friend and I no longer enjoyed each other's company, I'd ignore his/her phone calls, e-mails, or invitations.

Completely true   *Somewhat true/false*   *Completely false*

Mostly true   *Mostly false*

3 If my spouse or partner developed an annoying habit, I would threaten to leave unless he/she changed.

Completely true   *Somewhat true/false*   *Completely false*

Mostly true   *Mostly false*

4 If friends at work took credit for my work, I would get back at them by taking credit for something they did.

Completely true   *Somewhat true/false*   *Completely false*

Mostly true   *Mostly false*

5 If a friend borrowed something that has great sentimental value to me and failed to return it, I would cut off him/her without a word of explanation.

Completely true   *Somewhat true/false*   *Completely false*

Mostly true   *Mostly false*

6 If my date seemed ill at ease, I would decide there is no chemistry between the two of us and never call him/her again.

Completely true   *Somewhat true/false*   *Completely false*

Mostly true   *Mostly false*

7 If a friend at work was given the promotion I was angling for, I would tell myself I really didn't want that stupid promotion anyway.

Completely true   *Somewhat true/false*   *Completely false*

Mostly true   *Mostly false*

8 When a friend talks about another one of my friends behind his/her back, I join in.

Completely true   *Somewhat true/false*   *Completely false*

Mostly true   *Mostly false*

9 If my best friend says he/she has no time to socialize because of obligations at work, I would assume my friend doesn't like me anymore.

Completely true   *Somewhat true/false*   *Completely false*

Mostly true   *Mostly false*

10 If my best friend's lover has dumped him/her, I would worry that I might get dumped, too.

Completely true   *Somewhat true/false*   *Completely false*

Mostly true   *Mostly false*

SCORING ·······································

Each answer is awarded a specific number of points.

Completely true: *5 points*
Mostly true: *4 points*
Somewhat true/false: *3 points*
Mostly false: *2 points*
Completely false: *1 point*

50–40: You're the worst friend in history.
39–30: You're still not great friend material.
Below 30: You're the one to hang out with.

✏️ Are You a People Person?

① I try to comfort people who are upset or going through a difficult time.

Completely true   *Somewhat true/false*   *Completely false*

Mostly true   *Mostly false*

② If asked, I am happy to help a friend get organized.

Completely true   *Somewhat true/false*   *Completely false*

Mostly true   *Mostly false*

③ I am happiest among people I know very well.

Completely true   *Somewhat true/false*   *Completely false*

Mostly true   *Mostly false*

4 One of my favorite things is helping two people become friends.

Completely true   *Somewhat true/false*   *Completely false*

    Mostly true   *Mostly false*

5 If I help someone, I don't expect any kind of payment in return.

Completely true   *Somewhat true/false*   *Completely false*

    Mostly true   *Mostly false*

6 If someone helps me, I express my appreciation immediately.

Completely true   *Somewhat true/false*   *Completely false*

    Mostly true   *Mostly false*

7 I socialize with my friends as often as possible.

Completely true   *Somewhat true/false*   *Completely false*

    Mostly true   *Mostly false*

8 I enjoy volunteering in my community.

Completely true   *Somewhat true/false*   *Completely false*

    Mostly true   *Mostly false*

9 Conflict between people makes me uncomfortable.

Completely true   *Somewhat true/false*   *Completely false*

    Mostly true   *Mostly false*

10 I am always happy to help one of my neighbors.

Completely true   *Somewhat true/false*   *Completely false*

    Mostly true   *Mostly false*

SCORING ·

Each answer is awarded a specific number of points.

Completely true: *5 points*
Mostly true: *4 points*
Somewhat true/false: *3 points*
Mostly false: *2 points*
Completely false: *1 point*

50–40: You're well-adjusted and sympathetic.
39–30: More often than not, you're helpful and friendly.
Below 30: You're a borderline recluse.

✏️ Are You a Party Animal?

Mark the circle that corresponds to where on the continuum between each of the word/phrase pairs you fall. If you mark 1 or 5, then you identify most strongly with one of the words or phrases in the pair; 2 or 4 less so; 3 you are neutral.

1 boisterous ① • ② • ③ • ④ • ⑤ shy

2 chatty ① • ② • ③ • ④ • ⑤ quiet

3 outgoing ① • ② • ③ • ④ • ⑤ reserved

4 hands-on ① • ② • ③ • ④ • ⑤ hands off

5 center of attention ① • ② • ③ • ④ • ⑤ wallflower

6 dance ① • ② • ③ • ④ • ⑤ sit down

7 great wine ① • ② • ③ • ④ • ⑤ bottled water

8 tells jokes ① • ② • ③ • ④ • ⑤ doesn't get jokes

9 warm ① • ② • ③ • ④ • ⑤ remote

10 having fun ① • ② • ③ • ④ • ⑤ killing time

SCORING ·

50–40: Why were you even invited?
39–30: You're a borderline party pooper.
Below 30: People always invite you to the party, but they should probably take your car keys.

✐ How Good Are Your Manners?

1 In conversation, I rarely speak loudly.

Completely true   *Somewhat true/false*   *Completely false*

Mostly true   *Mostly false*

2 I rarely use foul language.

Completely true   *Somewhat true/false*   *Completely false*

Mostly true   *Mostly false*

3 I try to be respectful of elderly people.

Completely true   *Somewhat true/false*   *Completely false*

Mostly true   *Mostly false*

4 Even if I believe my opinion is important, I rarely interrupt a discussion.

Completely true   *Somewhat true/false*   *Completely false*

Mostly true   *Mostly false*

5 I never smack my lips or chew with my mouth open when eating.

Completely true   *Somewhat true/false*   *Completely false*

Mostly true   *Mostly false*

6 Usually I knock on the door before entering a room.

Completely true   *Somewhat true/false*   *Completely false*

Mostly true   *Mostly false*

7 Even if I can't find a trash barrel, I will not drop a candy wrapper or used tissue on the street.

Completely true   *Somewhat true/false*   *Completely false*

Mostly true   *Mostly false*

8 The words "please," "thank you," and "excuse me" are a basic part of my vocabulary.

Completely true   *Somewhat true/false*   *Completely false*

Mostly true   *Mostly false*

9 I try not to make noise in a church or a library.

Completely true   *Somewhat true/false*   *Completely false*

Mostly true   *Mostly false*

10 If something I've said or done offends someone else, then I apologize.

Completely true   *Somewhat true/false*   *Completely false*

Mostly true   *Mostly false*

SCORING ·····································

Each answer is awarded a specific number of points.

Completely true: 5 *points*
Mostly true: 4 *points*
Somewhat true/false: 3 *points*
Mostly false: 2 *points*
Completely false: 1 *point*

50–40: You're courteous and considerate.
39–30: More often than not, you're thoughtful.
Below 30: You're crass and insensitive.

✏️ Are You Neighborly?

1 I socialize with my neighbors.

    Completely true   *Somewhat true/false*   *Completely false*

        Mostly true   *Mostly false*

2 If my neighbor's dog got out, I'd try to bring him home.

    Completely true   *Somewhat true/false*   *Completely false*

        Mostly true   *Mostly false*

3 If I have a problem with one of my neighbors, I'd speak to him or about it politely.

    Completely true   *Somewhat true/false*   *Completely false*

        Mostly true   *Mostly false*

4 If I saw someone suspicious casing my neighbor's house, I'd call the police.

    Completely true   *Somewhat true/false*   *Completely false*

        Mostly true   *Mostly false*

5 I don't mind collecting my neighbors' mail while they are out of town.

Completely true   *Somewhat true/false*   *Completely false*

Mostly true   *Mostly false*

6 If the noise level of a neighbor's party got out of hand, I would walk over and ask them to keep it down.

Completely true   *Somewhat true/false*   *Completely false*

Mostly true   *Mostly false*

7 I'm cordial, even to neighbors I do not like.

Completely true   *Somewhat true/false*   *Completely false*

Mostly true   *Mostly false*

8 When a new family moves onto the block, I go over and introduce myself.

Completely true   *Somewhat true/false*   *Completely false*

Mostly true   *Mostly false*

9 If a neighbor is working outdoors and needs help, I offer my assistance.

Completely true   *Somewhat true/false*   *Completely false*

Mostly true   *Mostly false*

10 If I saw smoke coming from a neighbor's house, I would call 911, then run over to see if they were safe.

Completely true   *Somewhat true/false*   *Completely false*

Mostly true   *Mostly false*

SCORING ·····································

Each answer is awarded a specific number of points.

Completely true: 5 *points*
Mostly true: 4 *points*
Somewhat true/false: 3 *points*
Mostly false: 2 *points*
Completely false: 1 *point*

50–40: You're a beloved and valued member of the community.
39–30: You show signs of a neighborly spirit.
Below 30: You'll never win the neighborhood's Good
Samaritan Award.

CHAPTER 3

MIND VERSUS
EMOTIONS

Your emotions are important. They are a vital source of communication with others. A small child's laugh tells us that he or she feels happy and safe with us. A friend's look of anxiety is a call for help. And the confused expression on the face of stranger in the middle of a bustling city street is your opportunity to be a good Samaritan.

Just as important is the human mind, our capability to use our reason to think through problems. Our mind, our reason, our intelligence enable us to learn from past experiences and use what we have learned to respond successfully when we encounter new experiences.

Most of us go through life with a fairly well-balanced sense of when to respond to a situation emotionally and when to respond rationally. But there are individuals who tend to be ruled by their emotions or by their intellect. For example, let's say that your family gives you a new car for your birthday. You are filled with happiness, excitement, gratitude—all positive emotions, and this is the moment to let them out. An overly emotional person, however, might surrender to his or her impulses, jump into the car, and head off immediately on a cross-country road trip. An overly rational person might start quizzing his or her family about the details of the warranty.

Emotions and reason co-exist in every person. Some people may have a tendency to be overly emotional or overly analytical. There are even individuals who make a conscious choice to give free reign to their emotions—they believe it makes their responses to people and situations more authentic, while others all but suppress their emotions in favor of cool, detached, rational approach to life's experiences. Both extremes have a common problem—egotism. The extreme emotionalist and the extreme rationalist are so convinced that their way is the right way, that they have lost all sense of consideration for other people, who will probably be uncomfortable with the over-the-top emotions of the one and the cold analysis of the other.

Emotional Intelligence rejects extremes. The "Mind vs. Emotions" quizzes that follow are designed to help you identify how you respond to people and situations. If you find that you tend to be too emotional or too rational, you might want to consider ways that you can bring such tendencies into balance.

✏️ How Tough Are You Emotionally?

1 If someone else cries, I get teary.

    Completely true   *Somewhat true/false*   *Completely false*

        Mostly true   *Mostly false*

2 It's not unusual for me to share details of my personal life with strangers.

    Completely true   *Somewhat true/false*   *Completely false*

        Mostly true   *Mostly false*

3 An emotional movie can make me cry.

    Completely true   *Somewhat true/false*   *Completely false*

        Mostly true   *Mostly false*

4 Even after I've made a decision, my family and friends can persuade me to change my mind.

    Completely true   *Somewhat true/false*   *Completely false*

        Mostly true   *Mostly false*

5 If someone is rude to me, I feel bad for days afterward.

    Completely true   *Somewhat true/false*   *Completely false*

        Mostly true   *Mostly false*

6 My heart rules my head.

    Completely true   *Somewhat true/false*   *Completely false*

        Mostly true   *Mostly false*

7 I take offense easily.

Completely true   *Somewhat true/false*   *Completely false*

Mostly true   *Mostly false*

8 I tend to dwell on bad news.

Completely true   *Somewhat true/false*   *Completely false*

Mostly true   *Mostly false*

9 I often feel insecure.

Completely true   *Somewhat true/false*   *Completely false*

Mostly true   *Mostly false*

10 What my family, friends, and coworkers think of me is very important.

Completely true   *Somewhat true/false*   *Completely false*

Mostly true   *Mostly false*

SCORING ·

Each answer is awarded a specific number of points.

Completely true: *1 point*
Mostly true: *2 points*
Somewhat true/false: *3 points*
Mostly false: *4 points*
Completely false: *5 points*

50–40: You don't let emotions get the better of you.
39–30: You're somewhat in control of your emotions.
Below 30: You're an insccure, emotional wreck.

✐ How Impulsive Are You?

1 I'm usually the first person to answer the phone or the door.

Completely true   *Somewhat true/false*   *Completely false*

Mostly true   *Mostly false*

2 It is better to act on impulse than to analyze a situation thoroughly.

Completely true   *Somewhat true/false*   *Completely false*

Mostly true   *Mostly false*

3 My emotions guide my actions.

Completely true   *Somewhat true/false*   *Completely false*

Mostly true   *Mostly false*

4 Usually I rush through my work.

Completely true   *Somewhat true/false*   *Completely false*

Mostly true   *Mostly false*

5 I am not afraid to express my emotions or to say what's on my mind.

Completely true   *Somewhat true/false*   *Completely false*

Mostly true   *Mostly false*

6 Books of philosophy, economics, or other theoretical fields bore me.

Completely true   *Somewhat true/false*   *Completely false*

Mostly true   *Mostly false*

7 I like being the center of attention.

Completely true   *Somewhat true/false*   *Completely false*

Mostly true   *Mostly false*

8 I am willing to experiment and take risks.

Completely true   *Somewhat true/false*   *Completely false*

Mostly true   *Mostly false*

9 There are more important things in life than deadlines.

Completely true   *Somewhat true/false*   *Completely false*

Mostly true   *Mostly false*

10 I am adventurous.

Completely true   *Somewhat true/false*   *Completely false*

Mostly true   *Mostly false*

SCORING ·

Each answer is awarded a specific number of points.

Completely true: *5 points*
Mostly true: *4 points*
Somewhat true/false: *3 points*
Mostly false: *2 points*
Completely false: *1 point*

50–40: On a dare, you would bungee-jump off the Golden Gate Bridge.
39–30: Your impulses are somewhat under control.
Below 30: You're thoughtful—you look before you leap.

✏️ How Intellectual Are You?

1 Ideas interest me more than putting them to practical use.

Completely true   *Somewhat true/false*   *Completely false*

     Mostly true   *Mostly false*

2 I often contemplate the future of humankind.

Completely true   *Somewhat true/false*   *Completely false*

     Mostly true   *Mostly false*

3 I try to understand the mystery and complexity of life.

Completely true   *Somewhat true/false*   *Completely false*

     Mostly true   *Mostly false*

4 I need time to myself, especially after socializing.

Completely true   *Somewhat true/false*   *Completely false*

     Mostly true   *Mostly false*

5 Justice is more important than mercy.

Completely true   *Somewhat true/false*   *Completely false*

     Mostly true   *Mostly false*

6 Given a choice, I prefer to stay home and read a book than go to a party.

Completely true   *Somewhat true/false*   *Completely false*

     Mostly true   *Mostly false*

7 I avoid social obligations.

Completely true   *Somewhat true/false*   *Completely false*

     Mostly true   *Mostly false*

8 I cannot live or work in a noisy environment.

Completely true   *Somewhat true/false*   *Completely false*

Mostly true   *Mostly false*

9 Every situation in life can be improved if it is thoroughly analyzed.

Completely true   *Somewhat true/false*   *Completely false*

Mostly true   *Mostly false*

10 I have no trouble grasping new philosophical or scientific theories.

Completely true   *Somewhat true/false*   *Completely false*

Mostly true   *Mostly false*

SCORING ·

Each answer is awarded a specific number of points.

Completely true: *5 points*
Mostly true: *4 points*
Somewhat true/false: *3 points*
Mostly false: *2 points*
Completely false: *1 point*

50–40: You're cerebral and standoffish.
39–30: Your head and your heart seem to be working in balance.
Below 30: You're an emotional and thoughtless mess.

✐ What Type of Person Do You Admire?

Mark the circle that corresponds to where on the continuum between each of the word/phrase pairs you fall. If you mark 1 or 5, then you identify most strongly with one of the words or phrases in the pair; 2 or 4 less so; 3 you are neutral.

❶ technician ① • ② • ③ • ④ • ⑤ artist

❷ college professor ① • ② • ③ • ④ • ⑤ kindergarten teacher

❸ researcher ① • ② • ③ • ④ • ⑤ handyperson

❹ physicist ① • ② • ③ • ④ • ⑤ rancher

❺ mathematician ① • ② • ③ • ④ • ⑤ musician

❻ economist ① • ② • ③ • ④ • ⑤ dancer

❼ investor ① • ② • ③ • ④ • ⑤ consumer

❽ independently wealthy ① • ② • ③ • ④ • ⑤ entrepreneur

❾ dog breeder ① • ② • ③ • ④ • ⑤ dog owner

❿ theater critic ① • ② • ③ • ④ • ⑤ actor

SCORING ·

50–40: You're a hands-on, independent, artsy type.
39–30: You're artsy with a touch of brainiac go-getter.
Below 30: You're ambitious and cerebral.

✏️ Are You Cool and Detached?

1 I try to be impartial and fair-minded in my decisions.

Completely true   *Somewhat true/false*   *Completely false*

     Mostly true   *Mostly false*

2 Objective criticism of people and ideas is always a good thing.

Completely true   *Somewhat true/false*   *Completely false*

     Mostly true   *Mostly false*

3 Decisions should not be made on the basis of feelings.

Completely true   *Somewhat true/false*   *Completely false*

     Mostly true   *Mostly false*

4 I plan how I will spend each day.

Completely true   *Somewhat true/false*   *Completely false*

     Mostly true   *Mostly false*

5 In making a decision, I rely more on my own experiences that some abstract standard.

Completely true   *Somewhat true/false*   *Completely false*

     Mostly true   *Mostly false*

6 I like to put things in order.

Completely true   *Somewhat true/false*   *Completely false*

     Mostly true   *Mostly false*

7 I stick to my principles.

Completely true   *Somewhat true/false*   *Completely false*

     Mostly true   *Mostly false*

8 My workplace is usually neat and clean.

Completely true   *Somewhat true/false*   *Completely false*

     Mostly true   *Mostly false*

9 At work, I can see ways productivity could be improved.

Completely true   *Somewhat true/false*   *Completely false*

     Mostly true   *Mostly false*

10 Generally speaking, I can see how a particular event will play out.

Completely true   *Somewhat true/false*   *Completely false*

     Mostly true   *Mostly false*

SCORING ·

Each answer is awarded a specific number of points.

Completely true: *5 points*
Mostly true: *4 points*
Somewhat true/false: *3 points*
Mostly false: *2 points*
Completely false: *1 point*

50–40: You're completely dependable.
39–30: You're reliable in most situations.
Below 30: You're probably not at your best in an orderly work environment.

✏️ Are You an Extrovert?

❶ I do not get excited easily.

Completely true   *Somewhat true/false*   *Completely false*

Mostly true   *Mostly false*

❷ I do not reveal much about myself to other people.

Completely true   *Somewhat true/false*   *Completely false*

Mostly true   *Mostly false*

❸ At a party, I prefer to be at the periphery of the crowd, rather than in the center.

Completely true   *Somewhat true/false*   *Completely false*

Mostly true   *Mostly false*

❹ I enjoy taking long walks alone.

Completely true   *Somewhat true/false*   *Completely false*

Mostly true   *Mostly false*

❺ I am not comfortable talking about my feelings.

Completely true   *Somewhat true/false*   *Completely false*

Mostly true   *Mostly false*

❻ I prefer being with a small group of close friends rather than at a large party full of strangers.

Completely true   *Somewhat true/false*   *Completely false*

Mostly true   *Mostly false*

❼ I am most at ease with my family.

Completely true   *Somewhat true/false*   *Completely false*

Mostly true   *Mostly false*

8 I prefer following convention.

Completely true   *Somewhat true/false*   *Completely false*

      Mostly true   *Mostly false*

9 My habits are fairly consistent.

Completely true   *Somewhat true/false*   *Completely false*

      Mostly true   *Mostly false*

10 There are things about me that even my family does not know.

Completely true   *Somewhat true/false*   *Completely false*

      Mostly true   *Mostly false*

SCORING ·

Each answer is awarded a specific number of points.

Completely true: *5 points*
Mostly true: *4 points*
Somewhat true/false: *3 points*
Mostly false: *2 points*
Completely false: *1 point*

50–40: You keep most people at arm's length.
39–30: You're friendly, but you're never the life of the party.
Below 30: You're outgoing, and have genuine people skills.

✏ How Independent-Minded Are You?

1 Human existence may be meaningless.

Completely true   *Somewhat true/false*   *Completely false*

      Mostly true   *Mostly false*

2 I consider myself to be unconventional.

Completely true   *Somewhat true/false*   *Completely false*

      Mostly true   *Mostly false*

3 It is foolish for each generation to carry on their family, ethnic, and religious traditions.

Completely true   *Somewhat true/false*   *Completely false*

      Mostly true   *Mostly false*

4 I don't care what others think of me.

Completely true   *Somewhat true/false*   *Completely false*

      Mostly true   *Mostly false*

5 Intellectual curiosity is a prime motivating force in my life.

Completely true   *Somewhat true/false*   *Completely false*

      Mostly true   *Mostly false*

6 I enjoy avant-garde music.

Completely true   *Somewhat true/false*   *Completely false*

      Mostly true   *Mostly false*

7 Most of my opinions are not popular.

Completely true   *Somewhat true/false*   *Completely false*

      Mostly true   *Mostly false*

8 Living in a wealthy neighborhood would make me uncomfortable.

Completely true   *Somewhat true/false*   *Completely false*

Mostly true   *Mostly false*

9 There is nothing wrong with being outspoken.

Completely true   *Somewhat true/false*   *Completely false*

Mostly true   *Mostly false*

10 I consider myself to be an idealist.

Completely true   *Somewhat true/false*   *Completely false*

Mostly true   *Mostly false*

SCORING ·

Each answer is awarded a specific number of points.

Completely true: *5 points*
Mostly true: *4 points*
Somewhat true/false: *3 points*
Mostly false: *2 points*
Completely false: *1 point*

50–40: You're a borderline misanthrope.
39–30: You're independent-minded, but not obnoxiously so.
Below 30: You're conventional, but personable.

✏️ Are You a Brainiac?

1 Doing theoretical research all day would be my dream job.

Completely true   *Somewhat true/false*   *Completely false*

Mostly true   *Mostly false*

2 When others panic, I stay calm.

Completely true   *Somewhat true/false*   *Completely false*

Mostly true   *Mostly false*

3 Strong displays of emotion make me uncomfortable.

Completely true   *Somewhat true/false*   *Completely false*

Mostly true   *Mostly false*

4 Intellectual pursuits are my primary pastime.

Completely true   *Somewhat true/false*   *Completely false*

Mostly true   *Mostly false*

5 I often think about the purpose of my life.

Completely true   *Somewhat true/false*   *Completely false*

Mostly true   *Mostly false*

6 I want people to think of me as competent.

Completely true   *Somewhat true/false*   *Completely false*

Mostly true   *Mostly false*

7 I often use words and phrases most people do not understand.

Completely true   *Somewhat true/false*   *Completely false*

Mostly true   *Mostly false*

8 I have always been good at the sciences.

Completely true   *Somewhat true/false*   *Completely false*

       Mostly true   *Mostly false*

9 Detachment is an important character trait.

Completely true   *Somewhat true/false*   *Completely false*

       Mostly true   *Mostly false*

10 As a child, I was more comfortable with adults than with children my own age.

Completely true   *Somewhat true/false*   *Completely false*

       Mostly true   *Mostly false*

SCORING ·

Each answer is awarded a specific number of points.

Completely true: *5 points*
Mostly true: *4 points*
Somewhat true/false: *3 points*
Mostly false: *2 points*
Completely false: *1 point*

50–40: You will probably win a Nobel Prize.
39–30: You're smarter than average.
Below 30: You may have other positive qualities.

✏️ Do You Live in a Fantasy World?

1 People find me impressive.

Completely true   *Somewhat true/false*   *Completely false*

Mostly true   *Mostly false*

2 I spend most of my time pursuing one or two highly specialized interests.

Completely true   *Somewhat true/false*   *Completely false*

Mostly true   *Mostly false*

3 Someday I will be famous.

Completely true   *Somewhat true/false*   *Completely false*

Mostly true   *Mostly false*

4 I am an influential person.

Completely true   *Somewhat true/false*   *Completely false*

Mostly true   *Mostly false*

5 My family and friends don't do anything without seeking my advice.

Completely true   *Somewhat true/false*   *Completely false*

Mostly true   *Mostly false*

6 The jealousy of others has kept me from being more successful.

Completely true   *Somewhat true/false*   *Completely false*

Mostly true   *Mostly false*

7 I am interested in the paranormal.

Completely true   *Somewhat true/false*   *Completely false*

Mostly true   *Mostly false*

8 I am psychic.

Completely true   *Somewhat true/false*   *Completely false*

Mostly true   *Mostly false*

9 I am prophetic.

Completely true   *Somewhat true/false*   *Completely false*

Mostly true   *Mostly false*

10 I can relate to wizards.

Completely true   *Somewhat true/false*   *Completely false*

Mostly true   *Mostly false*

SCORING ·································

Each answer is awarded a specific number of points.

Completely true: *5 points*
Mostly true: *4 points*
Somewhat true/false: *3 points*
Mostly false: *2 points*
Completely false: *1 point*

50–40: You're seriously self-deluded.
39–30: You're quirky.
Below 30: You have remained in touch with reality.

✏️ Are You a Cynic or an Optimist?

❶ I don't know who I can trust.

Completely true   *Somewhat true/false*   *Completely false*

Mostly true   *Mostly false*

❷ I believe that, at heart, human beings only look out for Number One.

Completely true   *Somewhat true/false*   *Completely false*

Mostly true   *Mostly false*

❸ I believe people are getting nastier and more selfish.

Completely true   *Somewhat true/false*   *Completely false*

Mostly true   *Mostly false*

❹ Our elected officials only care about their jobs and their perks —they don't care about the ordinary citizens of this country.

Completely true   *Somewhat true/false*   *Completely false*

Mostly true   *Mostly false*

❺ Voting in local, state, and national elections is pointless.

Completely true   *Somewhat true/false*   *Completely false*

Mostly true   *Mostly false*

❻ Being happy and successful in life is a matter of luck. Nothing I do will change that.

Completely true   *Somewhat true/false*   *Completely false*

Mostly true   *Mostly false*

7 No one cares what happens to me.

Completely true   *Somewhat true/false*   *Completely false*

Mostly true   *Mostly false*

8 In our society, there are few opportunities for people to build happy, meaningful lives for themselves.

Completely true   *Somewhat true/false*   *Completely false*

Mostly true   *Mostly false*

9 Most people are irrational.

Completely true   *Somewhat true/false*   *Completely false*

Mostly true   *Mostly false*

10 Things will only get worse for the next generation.

Completely true   *Somewhat true/false*   *Completely false*

Mostly true   *Mostly false*

SCORING ·······································

Each answer is awarded a specific number of points.

Completely true: *5 points*
Mostly true: *4 points*
Somewhat true/false: *3 points*
Mostly false: *2 points*
Completely false: *1 point*

50–40: You're cranky, irritable, and bad-tempered.
39–30: You have bouts of cynicism and optimism.
Below 30: You always looks on the bright side of life.

CHAPTER 4

LOVE AND RELATIONSHIPS

Romance is complicated. It is fraught with so many emotions—love and desire, of course, but also uncertainty about commitment, fear of rejection, and disappointment if the relationship is not developing in the way you or your partner would like. Taking the cold analytical approach doesn't work—you can't dissect love like a laboratory frog. And surrendering entirely to emotions doesn't work either—at some point the people involved have to assess their chances of being a happy, successful couple. For these reasons, many experts in Emotional Intelligence consider romance the acid test of a person's EQ.

The key to having a loving relationship is coming from a loving home. If you grew up in a family that loved and supported and nurtured you, then the odds are excellent that you have the skills (for lack of a better word) to be a good romantic partner and eventually a good spouse.

Pity people who grew up in a dysfunctional family, where anger, violence, neglect, and abuse were routine. Thanks to the twisted lessons they learned about relationships, they have little chance of finding true love. But it is not hopeless: if they are willing to abandon those destructive ideas and habits, break the chain of dysfunctional relationships they witnessed as children and teenagers, and learn to be gentle and caring, then their chance of finding a loving partner increases substantially.

At the core of a healthy relationship is caring about the partner's happiness. In the most successful relationships, each partner wants the other to feel safe, content, appreciated, loved. If you are in such a relationship, you have been blessed. If you would like to find such a relationship, the "Love and Relationship" section may help. The quizzes encourage the qualities already present in your personality that demonstrate that you are good candidate for a serious relationship, or throw the spotlight on facets of your personality that may need some work.

✏️ Are You Ready for Love?

1 I often become infatuated with someone.

Completely true　　*Somewhat true/false*　　*Completely false*

Mostly true　　　　　*Mostly false*

2 I find it easy to say "I love you."

Completely true　　*Somewhat true/false*　　*Completely false*

Mostly true　　　　　*Mostly false*

3 I am at ease hugging men, women, and children.

Completely true　　*Somewhat true/false*　　*Completely false*

Mostly true　　　　　*Mostly false*

4 It has never been difficult for me to establish a long-term, loving relationship.

Completely true　　*Somewhat true/false*　　*Completely false*

Mostly true　　　　　*Mostly false*

5 I would require certain conditions in a relationship.

Completely true　　*Somewhat true/false*　　*Completely false*

Mostly true　　　　　*Mostly false*

6 A couple does not have to do everything together, or share the same opinions on every subject.

Completely true　　*Somewhat true/false*　　*Completely false*

Mostly true　　　　　*Mostly false*

7 I know I am worthy of love.

Completely true　　*Somewhat true/false*　　*Completely false*

Mostly true　　　　　*Mostly false*

8 When I'm alone with my romantic partner, I often experience intense feelings of sexual desire.

Completely true   *Somewhat true/false*   *Completely false*

        Mostly true   *Mostly false*

9 When I give a gift to my partner, I do not expect to receive one in return.

Completely true   *Somewhat true/false*   *Completely false*

        Mostly true   *Mostly false*

10 If my partner asked about my past relationships, I would be honest.

Completely true   *Somewhat true/false*   *Completely false*

        Mostly true   *Mostly false*

SCORING ·

Each answer is awarded a specific number of points.

Completely true: *5 points*
Mostly true: *4 points*
Somewhat true/false: *3 points*
Mostly false: *2 points*
Completely false: *1 point*

50–40: You're a keeper; anyone would be proud to take you home to meet the folks.
39–30: You're a pretty good bet.
Below 30: There are lots of good fish in the sea, so a prospective love interest might be seriously tempted to throw you back.

✏️ How Important Is Love in Your Life?

1 My main goal in life is to find my true love.

Completely true   *Somewhat true/false*   *Completely false*

    Mostly true   *Mostly false*

2 I do not like living alone.

Completely true   *Somewhat true/false*   *Completely false*

    Mostly true   *Mostly false*

3 I have been happiest when I have been in a relationship.

Completely true   *Somewhat true/false*   *Completely false*

    Mostly true   *Mostly false*

4 I am not afraid to let someone get close to me.

Completely true   *Somewhat true/false*   *Completely false*

    Mostly true   *Mostly false*

5 I want to raise a family.

Completely true   *Somewhat true/false*   *Completely false*

    Mostly true   *Mostly false*

6 I enjoy socializing.

Completely true   *Somewhat true/false*   *Completely false*

    Mostly true   *Mostly false*

7 I enjoy spending private time with the person I love.

Completely true   *Somewhat true/false*   *Completely false*

    Mostly true   *Mostly false*

8 It is important to me to be considerate of other people.

Completely true   *Somewhat true/false*   *Completely false*

Mostly true   *Mostly false*

9 I believe I am a loving person.

Completely true   *Somewhat true/false*   *Completely false*

Mostly true   *Mostly false*

10 I get somewhat depressed when I am not in a romantic relationship.

Completely true   *Somewhat true/false*   *Completely false*

Mostly true   *Mostly false*

SCORING ·

Each answer is awarded a specific number of points.

Completely true: *5 points*
Mostly true: *4 points*
Somewhat true/false: *3 points*
Mostly false: *2 points*
Completely false: *1 point*

50–40: For you, love cannot come along soon enough.
39–30: You're ready for love, but it's not critical.
Below 30: You probably won't have a date on New Year's Eve.

⬛⟩ Are You in the Mood for Love?

Mark the circle that corresponds to where on the continuum between each of the word/phrase pairs you fall. If you mark 1 or 5, then you identify most strongly with one of the words or phrases in the pair; 2 or 4 less so; 3 you are neutral.

1 go dancing ① • ② • ③ • ④ • ⑤ go to a hockey game

2 bouquet of flowers ① • ② • ③ • ④ • ⑤ fifth of vodka

3 romantic ① • ② • ③ • ④ • ⑤ formal

4 spontaneous ① • ② • ③ • ④ • ⑤ controlling

5 dinner for two ① • ② • ③ • ④ • ⑤ a night out with friends

6 ready to commit ① • ② • ③ • ④ • ⑤ reviewing options

7 affectionate ① • ② • ③ • ④ • ⑤ undemonstrative

8 courtship ① • ② • ③ • ④ • ⑤ friendship

9 bistro ① • ② • ③ • ④ • ⑤ food cart

10 St. Valentine's Day ① • ② • ③ • ④ • ⑤ St. Patrick's Day

SCORING ·································

50–40: You are not in the mood.
39–30: If you found love now, you could take it or leave it.
Below 30: Oh yeah, you are so in the mood.

✏️ Are You Over Your Ex?

1 Many times during the day I feel the urge to call my ex.

Completely true   *Somewhat true/false*   *Completely false*

Mostly true   *Mostly false*

2 The cards and gifts my ex gave me are special to me.

Completely true   *Somewhat true/false*   *Completely false*

Mostly true   *Mostly false*

3 I think of my ex often, especially when I am alone.

Completely true   *Somewhat true/false*   *Completely false*

Mostly true   *Mostly false*

4 Since the breakup, I have avoided my friends.

Completely true   *Somewhat true/false*   *Completely false*

Mostly true   *Mostly false*

5 I can't go to restaurants or theaters or parks I visited with my ex.

Completely true   *Somewhat true/false*   *Completely false*

Mostly true   *Mostly false*

6 It bothers me if my family or friends mention my ex in conversation.

Completely true   *Somewhat true/false*   *Completely false*

Mostly true   *Mostly false*

7 I often think of the good times I had with my ex.

Completely true   *Somewhat true/false*   *Completely false*

Mostly true   *Mostly false*

8 I am not ready for a new relationship.

Completely true   *Somewhat true/false*   *Completely false*

Mostly true   *Mostly false*

9 Sometimes I think the breakup was my fault.

Completely true   *Somewhat true/false*   *Completely false*

Mostly true   *Mostly false*

10 If my ex called, I would try to make up with him/her.

Completely true   *Somewhat true/false*   *Completely false*

Mostly true   *Mostly false*

SCORING ·

Each answer is awarded a specific number of points.

Completely true: *5 points*
Mostly true: *4 points*
Somewhat true/false: *3 points*
Mostly false: *2 points*
Completely false: *1 point*

50–40: You're so not over your ex.
39–30: You're getting there, but you're not over your ex yet.
Below 30: You're ready for the next, hopefully happier, relationship.

CHAPTER 5

THE HAPPINESS FACTOR

Emotionally intelligent people are happy people. Happy people have a loving family, a wide circle of friends and acquaintances. They work well with others, which makes them more productive at work and often leads them to do volunteer work in their communities. Happy people attract other people, they tend to be given more responsibility, and they are generally regarded as an asset in any organization to which they belong.

It's interesting to note that happy people are not all wealthy, nor are they all especially good looking, nor do they belong to the high-level professions. Wealth can vanish overnight; good looks fade over time; and holding on to a high-powered job can be a precarious business. Happy people know that these things are superficial and fleeting, so they ground their happiness in the things that last: family, friends, personal ethics, a generous spirit.

Why are happy people happy? Because they possess Emotional Intelligence. They are in control of their emotions, and they can assess and respond appropriately to the emotions of others. In other words, they have people skills.

Furthermore, happy people are not only productive, they are satisfied with their lives. This is not to say that every day is a day of fairy tale perfection for happy people—they have problems, challenges, sorrows, just like everyone else. But they love the people around them, and they are grateful for the blessings they already possess.

Unhappy people, on the other hand, tend to be aggressive, resentful, brimming over with negative emotions—particularly the feeling that they are unappreciated, not respected, and not being rewarded as they deserve. Not surprisingly, co-workers, neighbors, even family members find the chronically unhappy person unpleasant to be around.

The "Happiness Factor" quizzes that follow have been designed to measure your level of happiness with your life. A few of you will find that you are genuinely happy. And a few will confirm what you already knew—that you are just seething with dissatisfaction. But most who take these quizzes will fall in the middle, which gives you an opportunity to assess what you can do to become a happier, more contented person.

✐ Are You Happy?

1 I have a positive self-image.

Completely true   *Somewhat true/false*   *Completely false*

Mostly true   *Mostly false*

2 I make enough money to pay my bills and splurge on special things from time to time.

Completely true   *Somewhat true/false*   *Completely false*

Mostly true   *Mostly false*

3 My work is fulfilling.

Completely true   *Somewhat true/false*   *Completely false*

Mostly true   *Mostly false*

4 I enjoy one or two hobbies.

Completely true   *Somewhat true/false*   *Completely false*

Mostly true   *Mostly false*

5 I love my family.

Completely true   *Somewhat true/false*   *Completely false*

Mostly true   *Mostly false*

6 My life is satisfying.

Completely true   *Somewhat true/false*   *Completely false*

Mostly true   *Mostly false*

7 I make time to visit with my family and friends.

Completely true   *Somewhat true/false*   *Completely false*

Mostly true   *Mostly false*

8 I usually sleep well at night.

Completely true   *Somewhat true/false*   *Completely false*

Mostly true   *Mostly false*

9 I smile much more often than I frown.

Completely true   *Somewhat true/false*   *Completely false*

Mostly true   *Mostly false*

10 I have complaints from time to time, but I'm not a whiner.

Completely true   *Somewhat true/false*   *Completely false*

Mostly true   *Mostly false*

SCORING ··································

Each answer is awarded a specific number of points.

Completely true: *5 points*
Mostly true: *4 points*
Somewhat true/false: *3 points*
Mostly false: *2 points*
Completely false: *1 point*

50–40: You're a very happy person.
39–30: You're happy most of the time.
Below 30: You're the neighborhood grouch.

✏️ How Do You See Yourself?

Mark the circle that corresponds to where on the continuum between each of the word/phrase pairs you fall. If you mark 1 or 5, then you identify most strongly with one of the words or phrases in the pair; 2 or 4 less so; 3 you are neutral.

1 loser ① • ② • ③ • ④ • ⑤ winner

2 prestige does not bring happiness ① • ② • ③ • ④ • ⑤ prestige brings happiness

3 emotional ① • ② • ③ • ④ • ⑤ logical

4 instinct ① • ② • ③ • ④ • ⑤ facts

5 impulsive ① • ② • ③ • ④ • ⑤ analytical

6 outgoing ① • ② • ③ • ④ • ⑤ aloof

7 extravagant ① • ② • ③ • ④ • ⑤ cautious

8 conventional ① • ② • ③ • ④ • ⑤ unconventional

9 respect tradition ① • ② • ③ • ④ • ⑤ reject tradition

10 socially awkward ① • ② • ③ • ④ • ⑤ socially at ease

SCORING ··

50–40: You have a solid sense of self-esteem, plus you're thoughtful, sociable, and a bit of a free spirit.
39–30: You're balanced, with no extremes of behavior.
Below 30: You're nervous and ill at ease in almost all social situations.

✐ How Low Is Your Self-Esteem?

1 All it takes is one mistake and I berate myself as a stupid loser.

Completely true　　*Somewhat true/false*　　*Completely false*

Mostly true　　　　　*Mostly false*

2 Every time I strive for something, challenges and obstacles get in my way.

Completely true　　*Somewhat true/false*　　*Completely false*

Mostly true　　　　　*Mostly false*

3 I feel that doing my best is not good enough.

Completely true　　*Somewhat true/false*　　*Completely false*

Mostly true　　　　　*Mostly false*

4 I am fixated on my problems.

Completely true　　*Somewhat true/false*　　*Completely false*

Mostly true　　　　　*Mostly false*

5 Family, friends, work, and day-to-day life all bore me.

Completely true　　*Somewhat true/false*　　*Completely false*

Mostly true　　　　　*Mostly false*

6 I worry about things no one else worries about.

Completely true　　*Somewhat true/false*　　*Completely false*

Mostly true　　　　　*Mostly false*

7 The unhappiness of someone I love makes me unhappy, too.

Completely true　　*Somewhat true/false*　　*Completely false*

Mostly true　　　　　*Mostly false*

8 The opinions of other people can make me feel bad about myself.

Completely true　　　*Somewhat true/false*　　　*Completely false*

Mostly true　　　*Mostly false*

9 Nothing I've ever attempted has been a success.

Completely true　　　*Somewhat true/false*　　　*Completely false*

Mostly true　　　*Mostly false*

10 If someone does not praise my work, then I know it is no good.

Completely true　　　*Somewhat true/false*　　　*Completely false*

Mostly true　　　*Mostly false*

SCORING ·

Each answer is awarded a specific number of points.

Completely true: *5 points*
Mostly true: *4 points*
Somewhat true/false: *3 points*
Mostly false: *2 points*
Completely false: *1 point*

50–40: Your self-esteem is nonexistent.
39–30: Your self-esteem needs some work.
Below 30: You're capable and self-confident.

✏️ How Big of a Slacker Are You?

1 It's not unusual for me to put off work, chores, or errands.

Completely true   *Somewhat true/false*   *Completely false*

Mostly true   *Mostly false*

2 In school, if I didn't get around to studying, I cheated on my exams.

Completely true   *Somewhat true/false*   *Completely false*

Mostly true   *Mostly false*

3 I can lie around doing nothing for hours.

Completely true   *Somewhat true/false*   *Completely false*

Mostly true   *Mostly false*

4 Typically, I begin a task, like washing the dishes, then walk away before the job is done.

Completely true   *Somewhat true/false*   *Completely false*

Mostly true   *Mostly false*

5 Watching TV is my favorite activity.

Completely true   *Somewhat true/false*   *Completely false*

Mostly true   *Mostly false*

6 I rarely meet a deadline.

Completely true   *Somewhat true/false*   *Completely false*

Mostly true   *Mostly false*

7 If a task can be postponed, I will postpone it.

Completely true   *Somewhat true/false*   *Completely false*

Mostly true   *Mostly false*

8 Usually I am late for work.

Completely true   *Somewhat true/false*   *Completely false*

Mostly true   *Mostly false*

9 I would rather eat out than cook a meal.

Completely true   *Somewhat true/false*   *Completely false*

Mostly true   *Mostly false*

10 I like to sleep late in the morning.

Completely true   *Somewhat true/false*   *Completely false*

Mostly true   *Mostly false*

SCORING ·

Each answer is awarded a specific number of points.

Completely true: *5 points*
Mostly true: *4 points*
Somewhat true/false: *3 points*
Mostly false: *2 points*
Completely false: *1 point*

50–40: You're the king of the slackers.
39–30: You have lots of slacker potential.
Below 30: There's no time for you to be a slacker—you're too busy being productive.

✐ What Makes You Happy?

Mark the circle that corresponds to where on the continuum between each of the word/phrase pairs you fall. If you mark 1 or 5, then you identify most strongly with one of the words or phrases in the pair; 2 or 4 less so; 3 you are neutral.

1 sociable ① • ② • ③ • ④ • ⑤ solitary

2 family ① • ② • ③ • ④ • ⑤ coworkers

3 friends ① • ② • ③ • ④ • ⑤ acquaintances

4 home cooking ① • ② • ③ • ④ • ⑤ takeout

5 read a book ① • ② • ③ • ④ • ⑤ nap on the couch

6 volunteer ① • ② • ③ • ④ • ⑤ watch a movie

7 play with the kids ① • ② • ③ • ④ • ⑤ watch the game

8 help a neighbor ① • ② • ③ • ④ • ⑤ do it yourself

9 date night ① • ② • ③ • ④ • ⑤ channel surfing

10 bottle of wine ① • ② • ③ • ④ • ⑤ bag of chips

SCORING ································

50–40: You're a couch potato.
39–30: You appreciate at least some of the good things in life.
Below 30: You appreciate the good things in life.

✏ Are Your Emotions in Charge of You?

① Confronting someone who is angry terrifies me.

Completely true   *Somewhat true/false*   *Completely false*

Mostly true   *Mostly false*

② Hugging or kissing people makes me uncomfortable.

Completely true   *Somewhat true/false*   *Completely false*

Mostly true   *Mostly false*

③ I am self-conscious about my personal appearance or the way I behave around other people.

Completely true   *Somewhat true/false*   *Completely false*

Mostly true   *Mostly false*

④ I am afraid to let myself cry.

Completely true   *Somewhat true/false*   *Completely false*

Mostly true   *Mostly false*

⑤ If someone insults me, I dwell on the slight for days.

Completely true   *Somewhat true/false*   *Completely false*

Mostly true   *Mostly false*

⑥ A loss or a disappointment, even one that occurred many years ago, can make me profoundly sad.

Completely true   *Somewhat true/false*   *Completely false*

Mostly true   *Mostly false*

7 I get depressed easily.

Completely true　　　*Somewhat true/false*　　　*Completely false*

　　　　Mostly true　　　　　*Mostly false*

8 I often experience feelings of jealousy.

Completely true　　　*Somewhat true/false*　　　*Completely false*

　　　　Mostly true　　　　　*Mostly false*

9 A minor difficulty often makes me overreact.

Completely true　　　*Somewhat true/false*　　　*Completely false*

　　　　Mostly true　　　　　*Mostly false*

10 When I'm under pressure, I freak out.

Completely true　　　*Somewhat true/false*　　　*Completely false*

　　　　Mostly true　　　　　*Mostly false*

SCORING ································

Each answer is awarded a specific number of points.

Completely true: *5 points*
Mostly true: *4 points*
Somewhat true/false: *3 points*
Mostly false: *2 points*
Completely false: *1 point*

50–40: Your emotions are in charge.
39–30: Your emotions still have too much influence.
Below 30: Your emotions have learned there's a new sheriff in town.

✏️ How Impulsive Are You?

1 If I were unhappy at work, I would quit my job, even if I did not have another one lined up.

Completely true   *Somewhat true/false*   *Completely false*

Mostly true   *Mostly false*

2 On Friday afternoon, if a friend invited me to an all-expenses-paid weekend vacation, I would go.

Completely true   *Somewhat true/false*   *Completely false*

Mostly true   *Mostly false*

3 When I shop, it is not unusual for me to buy things I want but don't need.

Completely true   *Somewhat true/false*   *Completely false*

Mostly true   *Mostly false*

4 I would go skydiving if someone dared me.

Completely true   *Somewhat true/false*   *Completely false*

Mostly true   *Mostly false*

5 Sometimes, when I see an attractive stranger, I ask him/her out on a date.

Completely true   *Somewhat true/false*   *Completely false*

Mostly true   *Mostly false*

6 I have been known to go away for a weekend without telling my family what I'm doing.

Completely true   *Somewhat true/false*   *Completely false*

Mostly true   *Mostly false*

7 I would probably have a romantic fling if I knew my spouse wouldn't find out about it.

Completely true *Somewhat true/false* *Completely false*

Mostly true *Mostly false*

8 In high school, I played hooky about once a month.

Completely true *Somewhat true/false* *Completely false*

Mostly true *Mostly false*

9 I took my bonus and blew it all at the racetrack.

Completely true *Somewhat true/false* *Completely false*

Mostly true *Mostly false*

10 I hate a routine.

Completely true *Somewhat true/false* *Completely false*

Mostly true *Mostly false*

SCORING ·

Each answer is awarded a specific number of points.

Completely true: *5 points*
Mostly true: *4 points*
Somewhat true/false: *3 points*
Mostly false: *2 points*
Completely false: *1 point*

50–40: Impulsiveness guides your life.
39–30: You often surrender to impulse.
Below 30: You know the difference between spontaneity and impulsiveness.

CHAPTER 6

THE REAL YOU

If you were asked to describe your main quality, what would it be? Genuine? Impulsive? Reserved? Open? Do you worry too much? Are you a thrill seeker? Do you think of yourself as a confidant person? Do you find yourself all too often giving in to feelings of anger? How independent or unconventional are you?

Think of what gets you excited, what motivates you, what brings out your passion. Now try to understand why these things are so important to you. What do you get out of them? How do they make you feel? What is it about that feeling that you long to experience it again and again? This is an especially important exercise if you are indulging in negative experiences.

An essential step in increasing your emotional intelligence is to have a firm idea of the type of person you are. Of course, self-assessment can be tough—it is not much fun to confront your personal demons, to admit your shortcomings, but it is the only way to improve and to boost your EQ.

Daniel Goleman, the author of Emotional Intelligence, wrote, "Emotional Intelligence is the capacity for recognizing our own feelings." It is those feelings that compel us to bottle-up our emotions (perhaps out of fear of rejection?), to go sky-diving (because our day-to-day life is so unfulfilling?), or to enjoy the company of other people (which is a sign of sound Emotional Intelligence).

The following quizzes are intended to help you uncover the real you. If you have a tendency toward unhealthy emotions or unhelpful emotional responses, these quizzes may be useful in spotlighting them. And once you are aware of any emotional difficulties, you can take steps to correct them. Emotional Intelligence is most often defined as being sensitive to the emotional needs of others, but Emotional Intelligence is also about self-awareness, of being sensitive to your own emotional needs.

✏️ How Would You Describe Your Behavior?

Mark the circle that corresponds to where on the continuum between each of the word/phrase pairs you fall. If you mark 1 or 5, then you identify most strongly with one of the words or phrases in the pair; 2 or 4 less so; 3 you are neutral.

❶ genuine ① • ② • ③ • ④ • ⑤ false

❷ rational ① • ② • ③ • ④ • ⑤ impulsive

❸ spontaneous ① • ② • ③ • ④ • ⑤ structured

❹ prompt ① • ② • ③ • ④ • ⑤ tardy

❺ outgoing ① • ② • ③ • ④ • ⑤ standoffish

❻ caring ① • ② • ③ • ④ • ⑤ distant

❼ tidy ① • ② • ③ • ④ • ⑤ disorganized

❽ chatty ① • ② • ③ • ④ • ⑤ reserved

❾ prepare ① • ② • ③ • ④ • ⑤ improvise

❿ open ① • ② • ③ • ④ • ⑤ closed off

SCORING ·····································

50–40: You have impetuous tendencies, and no clue as to how to act around other people.

39–30: You have a few quirks, but you're still a good choice as a friend.

Below 30: You're balanced, grounded, probably fun to be around.

✏️ Are You Plagued by Anxiety?

1 People who know me consider me a very serious person.

Completely true   *Somewhat true/false*   *Completely false*

      Mostly true   *Mostly false*

2 When I'm away on vacation or a business trip, I think about my home often.

Completely true   *Somewhat true/false*   *Completely false*

      Mostly true   *Mostly false*

3 At night, it is often difficult for me to fall asleep.

Completely true   *Somewhat true/false*   *Completely false*

      Mostly true   *Mostly false*

4 Disappointing or making someone angry will bother for days or even weeks afterward.

Completely true   *Somewhat true/false*   *Completely false*

      Mostly true   *Mostly false*

5 I am extremely conscientious about all my responsibilities.

Completely true   *Somewhat true/false*   *Completely false*

      Mostly true   *Mostly false*

6 I hate it when I make a mistake.

Completely true   *Somewhat true/false*   *Completely false*

      Mostly true   *Mostly false*

7 When I leave the house, I often return to double-check that I have turned off the stove and securely locked the door.

Completely true   *Somewhat true/false*   *Completely false*

Mostly true   *Mostly false*

8 I avoid getting a physical because I worry that my doctor will find that I have a serious illness or condition.

Completely true   *Somewhat true/false*   *Completely false*

Mostly true   *Mostly false*

9 Among strangers, I feel self-conscious and uninteresting.

Completely true   *Somewhat true/false*   *Completely false*

Mostly true   *Mostly false*

10 If someone is not friendly to me, I worry that I offended him/her in some way.

Completely true   *Somewhat true/false*   *Completely false*

Mostly true   *Mostly false*

SCORING ·

Each answer is awarded a specific number of points.

Completely true: *5 points*
Mostly true: *4 points*
Somewhat true/false: *3 points*
Mostly false: *2 points*
Completely false: *1 point*

50–40: You're a nervous wreck.
39–30: You suffer from a bit too much anxiety.
Below 30: You're as cool and calm as a glass of water.

✏ Are You a Compulsive Thrill Seeker?

① When I was a child, I liked to steal things.

Completely true　　*Somewhat true/false*　　*Completely false*

Mostly true　　*Mostly false*

② I get bored easily.

Completely true　　*Somewhat true/false*　　*Completely false*

Mostly true　　*Mostly false*

③ I'm at my best in a big, noisy party.

Completely true　　*Somewhat true/false*　　*Completely false*

Mostly true　　*Mostly false*

④ In school, I often defied my teachers.

Completely true　　*Somewhat true/false*　　*Completely false*

Mostly true　　*Mostly false*

⑤ In stressful situations, I get headaches and become nauseous.

Completely true　　*Somewhat true/false*　　*Completely false*

Mostly true　　*Mostly false*

⑥ I'll often go away on vacation without telling my family and friends where I'm going.

Completely true　　*Somewhat true/false*　　*Completely false*

Mostly true　　*Mostly false*

⑦ The need for excitement has led me to do some crazy things.

Completely true　　*Somewhat true/false*　　*Completely false*

Mostly true　　*Mostly false*

8 I enjoy taking risks.

Completely true   *Somewhat true/false*   *Completely false*

     Mostly true   *Mostly false*

9 I enjoy reading thrillers.

Completely true   *Somewhat true/false*   *Completely false*

     Mostly true   *Mostly false*

10 If I haven't done something exciting or risky in a while, I become depressed.

Completely true   *Somewhat true/false*   *Completely false*

     Mostly true   *Mostly false*

SCORING ·

Each answer is awarded a specific number of points.

Completely true: *5 points*
Mostly true: *4 points*
Somewhat true/false: *3 points*
Mostly false: *2 points*
Completely false: *1 point*

50–40: You're a compulsive thrill seeker.
39–30: You're adventurous, but not insanely so.
Below 30: You know how to have a good time without risking a trip to the hospital, or jail.

✏️ How Self-Confident Are You?

1 At a restaurant, I add up the check and count my change.

Completely true *Somewhat true/false* *Completely false*

Mostly true *Mostly false*

2 It is impossible for me to start a conversation with a stranger.

Completely true *Somewhat true/false* *Completely false*

Mostly true *Mostly false*

3 My boss intimidates me.

Completely true *Somewhat true/false* *Completely false*

Mostly true *Mostly false*

4 I've had a hard life, but that has made me a stronger person.

Completely true *Somewhat true/false* *Completely false*

Mostly true *Mostly false*

5 No one thinks of me as assertive.

Completely true *Somewhat true/false* *Completely false*

Mostly true *Mostly false*

6 I never gamble.

Completely true *Somewhat true/false* *Completely false*

Mostly true *Mostly false*

7 It is difficult for me to get over times when I've screwed up.

Completely true *Somewhat true/false* *Completely false*

Mostly true *Mostly false*

8 I don't like my job, but I'm afraid a new job might turn out to be even worse.

Completely true   *Somewhat true/false*   *Completely false*

       Mostly true   *Mostly false*

9 Even among my friends, I rarely contribute much to a conversation.

Completely true   *Somewhat true/false*   *Completely false*

       Mostly true   *Mostly false*

10 I worry more than most people I know.

Completely true   *Somewhat true/false*   *Completely false*

       Mostly true   *Mostly false*

SCORING ·

Each answer is awarded a specific number of points.

Completely true: *5 points*
Mostly true: *4 points*
Somewhat true/false: *3 points*
Mostly false: *2 points*
Completely false: *1 point*

50–40: Your self-confidence is almost nil.
39–30: You have some self-confidence, but not very much.
Below 30: You're the mayor of Self-Confidence Town.

✎ Are You an Angry Person?

1 I don't like it when people tell me what to do.

Completely true   *Somewhat true/false*   *Completely false*

       Mostly true   *Mostly false*

2 There is nothing wrong with standing up to authority figures, such as a police officer.

Completely true   *Somewhat true/false*   *Completely false*

       Mostly true   *Mostly false*

3 I like to be in charge.

Completely true   *Somewhat true/false*   *Completely false*

       Mostly true   *Mostly false*

4 If someone has hurt or offended me, I plot how to get even.

Completely true   *Somewhat true/false*   *Completely false*

       Mostly true   *Mostly false*

5 If someone is bothering me, I let him/her know about it.

Completely true   *Somewhat true/false*   *Completely false*

       Mostly true   *Mostly false*

6 Modest people get walked on.

Completely true   *Somewhat true/false*   *Completely false*

       Mostly true   *Mostly false*

7 It's healthy to release your anger.

Completely true   *Somewhat true/false*   *Completely false*

       Mostly true   *Mostly false*

8 I find it very satisfying to tell off an obnoxious person.

Completely true   *Somewhat true/false*   *Completely false*

     Mostly true   *Mostly false*

9 If people don't like it when I express my anger, that's their problem.

Completely true   *Somewhat true/false*   *Completely false*

     Mostly true   *Mostly false*

10 What other people think of me doesn't concern me at all.

Completely true   *Somewhat true/false*   *Completely false*

     Mostly true   *Mostly false*

SCORING ·

Each answer is awarded a specific number of points.

Completely true: *5 points*
Mostly true: *4 points*
Somewhat true/false: *3 points*
Mostly false: *2 points*
Completely false: *1 point*

50–40: You're a ticking time bomb.
39–30: You're still way too angry.
Below 30: You have your anger under control.

✏️ Are You Lonely?

1 I get lonely if I am not living with a roommate, lover, or spouse.

Completely true   *Somewhat true/false*   *Completely false*

    Mostly true   *Mostly false*

2 I believe that if I were more successful in my career, I would never be lonely.

Completely true   *Somewhat true/false*   *Completely false*

    Mostly true   *Mostly false*

3 When I run into my neighbors, I never know what to say.

Completely true   *Somewhat true/false*   *Completely false*

    Mostly true   *Mostly false*

4 I feel awkward and uncomfortable when I must speak to a stranger, such as a waiter or a sales clerk.

Completely true   *Somewhat true/false*   *Completely false*

    Mostly true   *Mostly false*

5 It seems to me that today most people keep to themselves, so it's harder to make new friends.

Completely true   *Somewhat true/false*   *Completely false*

    Mostly true   *Mostly false*

6 I think of myself as shy.

Completely true   *Somewhat true/false*   *Completely false*

    Mostly true   *Mostly false*

7 Office parties and other large social functions make me ill at ease.

Completely true   *Somewhat true/false*   *Completely false*

Mostly true   *Mostly false*

8 I have a few close friends, but I'm not sure how to make more.

Completely true   *Somewhat true/false*   *Completely false*

Mostly true   *Mostly false*

9 I get bored sitting at home evening after evening.

Completely true   *Somewhat true/false*   *Completely false*

Mostly true   *Mostly false*

10 I would like to have a more active social life.

Completely true   *Somewhat true/false*   *Completely false*

Mostly true   *Mostly false*

S C O R I N G ·

Each answer is awarded a specific number of points.

Completely true: *5 points*
Mostly true: *4 points*
Somewhat true/false: *3 points*
Mostly false: *2 points*
Completely false: *1 point*

50–40: You're the living, breathing definition of lonely.
39–30: You need to get out more.
Below 30: You're rarely, if ever, lonely.

✐ How Conventional Are You?

Mark the circle that corresponds to where on the continuum between each of the word/phrase pairs you fall. If you mark 1 or 5, then you identify most strongly with one of the words or phrases in the pair; 2 or 4 less so; 3 you are neutral.

1 innovate ① • ② • ③ • ④ • ⑤ preserve the status quo

2 atheist ① • ② • ③ • ④ • ⑤ theist

3 individualistic ① • ② • ③ • ④ • ⑤ group-oriented

4 change ① • ② • ③ • ④ • ⑤ tradition

5 militant ① • ② • ③ • ④ • ⑤ authoritarian

6 free-form ① • ② • ③ • ④ • ⑤ structured

7 rebellious ① • ② • ③ • ④ • ⑤ dutiful

8 abstract ① • ② • ③ • ④ • ⑤ concrete

9 defiant ① • ② • ③ • ④ • ⑤ obedient

10 doubt ① • ② • ③ • ④ • ⑤ faith

SCORING ·

50–40: There's no chance of your becoming a rebel.
39–30: You dabble in nonconformity from time to time.
Below 30: You're the classic nonconformist.

✏️ How Independent Are You?

① I like to join organizations.

Completely true   *Somewhat true/false*   *Completely false*

Mostly true   *Mostly false*

② I prefer to make household and auto repairs myself.

Completely true   *Somewhat true/false*   *Completely false*

Mostly true   *Mostly false*

③ I consider myself to be self-reliant.

Completely true   *Somewhat true/false*   *Completely false*

Mostly true   *Mostly false*

④ When I make a mistake, I admit it; I don't make excuses.

Completely true   *Somewhat true/false*   *Completely false*

Mostly true   *Mostly false*

⑤ Other people's opinion of me does not matter.

Completely true   *Somewhat true/false*   *Completely false*

Mostly true   *Mostly false*

⑥ I am not afraid to express an opinion that is contrary to what my family and friends believe.

Completely true   *Somewhat true/false*   *Completely false*

Mostly true   *Mostly false*

⑦ It is an admirable thing to swim against the current.

Completely true   *Somewhat true/false*   *Completely false*

Mostly true   *Mostly false*

8 I am not self-conscious.

Completely true   *Somewhat true/false*   *Completely false*

      Mostly true   *Mostly false*

9 Change does not upset me.

Completely true   *Somewhat true/false*   *Completely false*

      Mostly true   *Mostly false*

10 I love my family and friends, but I am not emotionally needy.

Completely true   *Somewhat true/false*   *Completely false*

      Mostly true   *Mostly false*

SCORING ································

Each answer is awarded a specific number of points.

Completely true: *5 points*
Mostly true: *4 points*
Somewhat true/false: *3 points*
Mostly false: *2 points*
Completely false: *1 point*

50–40: You're independent, with lots of self-sufficiency to spare.
39–30: You're a straight shooter.
Below 30: Maybe you're not needy, but you're certainly not independent.

CHAPTER 7

ALL IN THE
FAMILY

John Lennon assured us, "All you need is love." Well, in family life love is vital, but it's not all you need. You also need kindness, respect, support, encouragement, patience (lots of patience), and tolerance. And when we say tolerance, we mean it in the old-fashioned sense of "to put up with." The most successful families put up with a lot from each—divergent interests; different tastes in clothing, music, and friends; conflicting opinions on politics, religion, sexuality, and all those other hot-button issues that can set off a ferocious argument around the dinner table. Parents and children, brothers and sisters, have to find some way to put up with one another's irritating habits and annoying opinions by remembering what is essential: they are a family, and they love each other.

Psychologist Maurice Elias suggests that a family take the "neighbor test." Imagine that the entire family is in the middle of a full-blown argument when the door bell rings. A neighbor has come by to visit. What will the family do? In most circumstances, they will be welcoming, friendly, and hospitable to their unexpected guest. Everyone trots out their company manners, and the visit is a lovely time for all. Eventually the neighbor goes home, and Elias asks, "What happens next?" In the worst case, the family picks up the brawl where they left off. But in most cases, the visit has broken the tension and the family returns to its routine and usual civil interaction.

Why did the family end their argument and become pleasant when the neighbor showed up on the doorstep? Because they did not want to expose themselves to neighborhood gossip as "the angry family," or make a friend uncomfortable in their home. They did this by exercising a quality they all possessed—adults, teens, children—and that quality is self-control. Dr. Elias identifies self-control as an important quality for the emotional intelligence of a family, and he urges parents and kids to exercise it at least one day a week by not saying anything to one another that they wouldn't say if a neighbor were in the room.

The "All in the Family" quizzes help you explore your skills as a parent, your preparedness for getting through the kids' teen years, and even the state of your marriage—because family life is much happier if the spark is still there.

✐ How Are Your Parenting Skills?

1 Just the thought of discussing sex, drugs, and alcohol with my kids makes me uncomfortable.

Completely true   *Somewhat true/false*   *Completely false*

Mostly true   *Mostly false*

2 My love for my kids changes depending on how they behave.

Completely true   *Somewhat true/false*   *Completely false*

Mostly true   *Mostly false*

3 Making any demands on young children will make them anxious when they grow older.

Completely true   *Somewhat true/false*   *Completely false*

Mostly true   *Mostly false*

4 Sometimes a spanking is the only way to control a child.

Completely true   *Somewhat true/false*   *Completely false*

Mostly true   *Mostly false*

5 If my children misbehave, I correct them at once even if their friends are present.

Completely true   *Somewhat true/false*   *Completely false*

Mostly true   *Mostly false*

6 I'd rather my kids thought of me as their friend than their parent.

Completely true   *Somewhat true/false*   *Completely false*

Mostly true   *Mostly false*

7 Being an authority figure is important. Even if I make an obvious mistake, I do not apologize to my kids.

Completely true　　　*Somewhat true/false*　　　*Completely false*

Mostly true　　　*Mostly false*

8 Children must be permitted to make their own mistakes and learn from them.

Completely true　　　*Somewhat true/false*　　　*Completely false*

Mostly true　　　*Mostly false*

9 There are some subjects I will not discuss with my kids.

Completely true　　　*Somewhat true/false*　　　*Completely false*

Mostly true　　　*Mostly false*

10 If my child is having trouble with another child at school, it's the school's responsibility to sort it out.

Completely true　　　*Somewhat true/false*　　　*Completely false*

Mostly true　　　*Mostly false*

SCORING ·

Each answer is awarded a specific number of points.

Completely true: *5 points*
Mostly true: *4 points*
Somewhat true/false: *3 points*
Mostly false: *2 points*
Completely false: *1 point*

50–40: You're completely clueless about raising a child.
39–30: You still need serious guidance about how to be a parent.
Below 30: You're the kind of parent you see in 1960s sitcoms.

✏️ Which Word or Phrase Best Describes Your Child?

Mark the circle that corresponds to where on the continuum between each of the word/phrase pairs you fall. If you mark 1 or 5, then you identify most strongly with one of the words or phrases in the pair; 2 or 4 less so; 3 you are neutral.

1 outgoing ① • ② • ③ • ④ • ⑤ unsociable

2 in high spirits ① • ② • ③ • ④ • ⑤ unhappy

3 curious ① • ② • ③ • ④ • ⑤ bored

4 generous ① • ② • ③ • ④ • ⑤ stingy

5 affectionate ① • ② • ③ • ④ • ⑤ standoffish

6 talkative ① • ② • ③ • ④ • ⑤ restrained

7 kind ① • ② • ③ • ④ • ⑤ mean

8 thoughtful ① • ② • ③ • ④ • ⑤ selfish

9 imaginative ① • ② • ③ • ④ • ⑤ irritable

10 loving ① • ② • ③ • ④ • ⑤ withdrawn

SCORING ·······································

50–40: Get help now.
39–30: You raised a good kid with lots of potential.
Below 30: You have a happy, well-adjusted kid—keep up the good work.

✏️ Who's Responsible for the Kids?

1 Raising the children is primarily the mother's responsibility.

Completely true　　*Somewhat true/false*　　*Completely false*

Mostly true　　*Mostly false*

2 After working all day, the father should not be expected to take care of the kids.

Completely true　　*Somewhat true/false*　　*Completely false*

Mostly true　　*Mostly false*

3 If a woman has a career, her family will suffer.

Completely true　　*Somewhat true/false*　　*Completely false*

Mostly true　　*Mostly false*

4 Women are more nurturing than men.

Completely true　　*Somewhat true/false*　　*Completely false*

Mostly true　　*Mostly false*

5 Most fathers don't know how to care for children.

Completely true　　*Somewhat true/false*　　*Completely false*

Mostly true　　*Mostly false*

6 Parents who send their kids to day care and preschool are letting strangers raise their children.

Completely true　　*Somewhat true/false*　　*Completely false*

Mostly true　　*Mostly false*

7 Children sent to day care develop emotional problems later in life.

Completely true   *Somewhat true/false*   *Completely false*

Mostly true   *Mostly false*

8 If children are sick, their mother should stay home from work to take care of them.

Completely true   *Somewhat true/false*   *Completely false*

Mostly true   *Mostly false*

9 Fathers are clumsy when it comes to changing a diaper or feeding a baby.

Completely true   *Somewhat true/false*   *Completely false*

Mostly true   *Mostly false*

10 Children who come from homes where both parents work are more likely to become delinquents.

Completely true   *Somewhat true/false*   *Completely false*

Mostly true   *Mostly false*

SCORING ·

Each answer is awarded a specific number of points.

Completely true: *5 points*
Mostly true: *4 points*
Somewhat true/false: *3 points*
Mostly false: *2 points*
Completely false: *1 point*

50–40: You exemplify the Stone Age approach to family life and child rearing.

39–30: You're still a little hidebound when it comes to gender roles. **Below 30:** You have a flexible, cooperative, shared approach to raising the kids.

✐ How Well Do You Understand Teenagers?

1 Teens have real feelings that should be acknowledged and respected.

Completely true   *Somewhat true/false*   *Completely false*

Mostly true   *Mostly false*

2 Even if your teens are moody, they still want to know you love them.

Completely true   *Somewhat true/false*   *Completely false*

Mostly true   *Mostly false*

3 Teens will respect and accept limits on their actions, such as curfews and deadlines, as long as they are reasonable.

Completely true   *Somewhat true/false*   *Completely false*

Mostly true   *Mostly false*

4 Not all teens are rebellious all the time.

Completely true   *Somewhat true/false*   *Completely false*

Mostly true   *Mostly false*

5 Parents should make their teen's friends welcome in their home.

Completely true   *Somewhat true/false*   *Completely false*

Mostly true   *Mostly false*

6 In high school, young people need more freedom than they had in grammar school.

Completely true   *Somewhat true/false*   *Completely false*

Mostly true   *Mostly false*

7 There is nothing wrong with telling teens to get a job so they have their own spending money.

Completely true   *Somewhat true/false*   *Completely false*

Mostly true   *Mostly false*

8 If you talk honestly about sex and drugs with your teens, they will probably listen.

Completely true   *Somewhat true/false*   *Completely false*

Mostly true   *Mostly false*

9 Teens do not respect parents who are hypocritical.

Completely true   *Somewhat true/false*   *Completely false*

Mostly true   *Mostly false*

10 Family dinners are an excellent way to keep up with what your teen is doing.

Completely true   *Somewhat true/false*   *Completely false*

Mostly true   *Mostly false*

SCORING ·

Each answer is awarded a specific number of points.

Completely true: *5 points*
Mostly true: *4 points*
Somewhat true/false: *3 points*

Mostly false: 2 points
Completely false: 1 point

50–40: You could teach a course on raising teens.
39–30: Overall, you have good teen-raising skills.
Below 30: The teen years are going to be long and ugly in your household.

✐ How Well Do You Know Your Spouse?

1 My spouse's bad moods mystify me—I don't know what sets them off.

Completely true　　*Somewhat true/false*　　*Completely false*

　　Mostly true　　　　　　*Mostly false*

2 I never know what type of gift to give my spouse.

Completely true　　*Somewhat true/false*　　*Completely false*

　　Mostly true　　　　　　*Mostly false*

3 My spouse wouldn't be interested in a regular date night.

Completely true　　*Somewhat true/false*　　*Completely false*

　　Mostly true　　　　　　*Mostly false*

4 My spouse loves taking care of the kids.

Completely true　　*Somewhat true/false*　　*Completely false*

　　Mostly true　　　　　　*Mostly false*

5 I know the month of my spouse's birthday, but not the date.

Completely true　　*Somewhat true/false*　　*Completely false*

　　Mostly true　　　　　　*Mostly false*

6 Neither my spouse nor I care much about our personal appearance.

Completely true　　　*Somewhat true/false*　　　*Completely false*

　　　　Mostly true　　　　　*Mostly false*

7 Compliments and spontaneous little gifts are for when you're dating.

Completely true　　　*Somewhat true/false*　　　*Completely false*

　　　　Mostly true　　　　　*Mostly false*

8 My spouse knows I love him/her. There's no need to say it out loud.

Completely true　　　*Somewhat true/false*　　　*Completely false*

　　　　Mostly true　　　　　*Mostly false*

9 Making my in-laws feel like they are part of our family doesn't interest me.

Completely true　　　*Somewhat true/false*　　　*Completely false*

　　　　Mostly true　　　　　*Mostly false*

10 Sometimes I say something critical about my spouse in front of the kids.

Completely true　　　*Somewhat true/false*　　　*Completely false*

　　　　Mostly true　　　　　*Mostly false*

SCORING ·

Each answer is awarded a specific number of points.

Completely true: *5 points*
Mostly true: *4 points*

Somewhat true/false: *3 points*
Mostly false: *2 points*
Completely false: *1 point*

50–40: You're a troglodyte.
39–30: You need work on your relationship skills.
Below 30: You're a fully evolved human being.

✏️ Are You Ready to Introduce Your Kids to the Social Network?

1 When my children express an interest in social networks, I'll introduce them to social networking sites.

Completely true *Somewhat true/false* *Completely false*

Mostly true *Mostly false*

2 When the kids are young, I'll monitor their social networking activity.

Completely true *Somewhat true/false* *Completely false*

Mostly true *Mostly false*

3 I've told my kids that what is bad offline is bad online.

Completely true *Somewhat true/false* *Completely false*

Mostly true *Mostly false*

4 I've set daily limits on how long the kids can be on a social networking site.

Completely true *Somewhat true/false* *Completely false*

Mostly true *Mostly false*

5 I talk about the sites with my kids to show that I'm interested in their online activities.

Completely true   *Somewhat true/false*   *Completely false*

Mostly true   *Mostly false*

6 My kids cannot join a site that requires their full name, date of birth, or the name of their school.

Completely true   *Somewhat true/false*   *Completely false*

Mostly true   *Mostly false*

7 I have installed safety controls on all our online devices so there are sites the kids are automatically barred from visiting.

Completely true   *Somewhat true/false*   *Completely false*

Mostly true   *Mostly false*

8 I've directed my kids to kid-centric sites.

Completely true   *Somewhat true/false*   *Completely false*

Mostly true   *Mostly false*

9 I spend time online with my kids.

Completely true   *Somewhat true/false*   *Completely false*

Mostly true   *Mostly false*

10 I have the final say on which site(s) my kids can sign onto.

Completely true   *Somewhat true/false*   *Completely false*

Mostly true   *Mostly false*

SCORING ·······································

Each answer is awarded a specific number of points.

Completely true: 5 *points*
Mostly true: 4 *points*
Somewhat true/false: 3 *points*
Mostly false: 2 *points*
Completely false: 1 *point*

50–40: Yours is a safe, sane approach to introducing kids to social networking.
39–30: You have some good ideas, but should adopt a few more.
Below 30: You're just asking for trouble.

✏ Is There Still a Spark in Your Marriage?

1 My spouse and I kiss all the time.

Completely true   *Somewhat true/false*   *Completely false*
          Mostly true   *Mostly false*

2 We find ways to spend time alone.

Completely true   *Somewhat true/false*   *Completely false*
          Mostly true   *Mostly false*

3 We have regular date nights.

Completely true   *Somewhat true/false*   *Completely false*
          Mostly true   *Mostly false*

4 Sometimes our parents take the kids for a weekend so we can be alone.

Completely true   *Somewhat true/false*   *Completely false*

Mostly true   *Mostly false*

5 We say "I love you" just about every day.

Completely true   *Somewhat true/false*   *Completely false*

Mostly true   *Mostly false*

6 My spouse is sexy.

Completely true   *Somewhat true/false*   *Completely false*

Mostly true   *Mostly false*

7 I'm not interested in anyone else.

Completely true   *Somewhat true/false*   *Completely false*

Mostly true   *Mostly false*

8 We take care of each other.

Completely true   *Somewhat true/false*   *Completely false*

Mostly true   *Mostly false*

9 My life would be diminished without my spouse.

Completely true   *Somewhat true/false*   *Completely false*

Mostly true   *Mostly false*

10 This is the person I'll spend the rest of my life with.

Completely true   *Somewhat true/false*   *Completely false*

Mostly true   *Mostly false*

SCORING ·····································

Each answer is awarded a specific number of points.

Completely true: 5 *points*
Mostly true: 4 *points*
Somewhat true/false: 3 *points*
Mostly false: 2 *points*
Completely false: 1 *point*

50–40: Yours is a grade-A marriage.
39–30: You're still a good match.
Below 30: Make an appointment with a marriage counselor now.

✏ Is Your Birth Order Having an Impact on Your Life?

❶ Growing up, my brothers and sisters played together all the time. Sometimes we bickered, but for the most part we had fun.

Completely true   *Somewhat true/false*   *Completely false*

Mostly true   *Mostly false*

❷ My parents spoiled my youngest sibling, but they didn't overdo it.

Completely true   *Somewhat true/false*   *Completely false*

Mostly true   *Mostly false*

❸ If my mother had a favorite child, none of us could tell.

Completely true   *Somewhat true/false*   *Completely false*

Mostly true   *Mostly false*

④ I don't believe my parents expected more of their eldest child.

Completely true　　　*Somewhat true/false*　　　*Completely false*

Mostly true　　　*Mostly false*

⑤ All of my siblings and I excel at different things.

Completely true　　　*Somewhat true/false*　　　*Completely false*

Mostly true　　　*Mostly false*

⑥ None of my siblings would ever try to steal my boyfriend/girlfriend.

Completely true　　　*Somewhat true/false*　　　*Completely false*

Mostly true　　　*Mostly false*

⑦ Sometimes we are competitive, but we are never jealous of each other.

Completely true　　　*Somewhat true/false*　　　*Completely false*

Mostly true　　　*Mostly false*

⑧ The idea that birth order can influence how you develop as a person is a myth.

Completely true　　　*Somewhat true/false*　　　*Completely false*

Mostly true　　　*Mostly false*

⑨ The most important factor in personal development is coming from a loving, supportive, and understanding family.

Completely true　　　*Somewhat true/false*　　　*Completely false*

Mostly true　　　*Mostly false*

⑩ A little sibling rivalry is healthy—it convinced us to always try our best.

Completely true　　　*Somewhat true/false*　　　*Completely false*

Mostly true　　　*Mostly false*

SCORING ··

Each answer is awarded a specific number of points.

Completely true: *5 points*
Mostly true: *4 points*
Somewhat true/false: *3 points*
Mostly false: *2 points*
Completely false: *1 point*

50-40: Birth order is meaningless to you.
39-30: A little tension is detected, but it's not out of control.
Below 30: Isn't it time to give up those resentments from childhood?

✏️ How Well Do You Get Along with Your Parents?

1 You live near your parents and visit them almost daily.

Completely true   *Somewhat true/false*   *Completely false*
     Mostly true   *Mostly false*

2 You invite your parents to just about every social event you are hosting.

Completely true   *Somewhat true/false*   *Completely false*
     Mostly true   *Mostly false*

3 You speak with your parents on the phone every day.

Completely true   *Somewhat true/false*   *Completely false*
     Mostly true   *Mostly false*

4 You spend your vacation with your parents and immediate family.

Completely true   *Somewhat true/false*   *Completely false*

Mostly true   *Mostly false*

5 You would give up a boyfriend/girlfriend—even you truly loved him/her—if your parents didn't like him/her.

Completely true   *Somewhat true/false*   *Completely false*

Mostly true   *Mostly false*

6 Your parents know all your friends, all your workplace colleagues, all your neighbors.

Completely true   *Somewhat true/false*   *Completely false*

Mostly true   *Mostly false*

7 Before making even minor decisions, such as purchasing new furniture or a new appliance, you ask your parents for their opinion.

Completely true   *Somewhat true/false*   *Completely false*

Mostly true   *Mostly false*

8 Your parents' approval is very important to you.

Completely true   *Somewhat true/false*   *Completely false*

Mostly true   *Mostly false*

9 If your parents go out of town for any period of time, you miss them terribly.

Completely true   *Somewhat true/false*   *Completely false*

Mostly true   *Mostly false*

10 Your friends have commented on how much time you spend with your parents and have expressed concern that you might be too dependent on them.

Completely true   *Somewhat true/false*   *Completely false*

Mostly true   *Mostly false*

SCORING ·······································

Each answer is awarded a specific number of points.

Completely true: *5 points*
Mostly true: *4 points*
Somewhat true/false: *3 points*
Mostly false: *2 points*
Completely false: *1 point*

50-40: You and your parents are grown-ups.
39-30: You have a tight bond with your parents, but not in an unhealthy way.
Below 30: Hopelessly clingy.

✏ How Healthy Is Your Mother-Daughter Relationship?

1 My mother/daughter respects and understands me.

Completely true   *Somewhat true/false*   *Completely false*

Mostly true   *Mostly false*

2 When ever I think of my mother/daughter, I am filled with feelings of love and affection.

Completely true　　*Somewhat true/false*　　*Completely false*

　　　　Mostly true　　　　*Mostly false*

3 My mother/daughter may not always agree with me, but she supports my decisions.

Completely true　　*Somewhat true/false*　　*Completely false*

　　　　Mostly true　　　　*Mostly false*

4 I can have serious, heart-to-heart discussions with my mother/daughter.

Completely true　　*Somewhat true/false*　　*Completely false*

　　　　Mostly true　　　　*Mostly false*

5 I visit with my mother/daughter fairly often, but we respect each other's privacy, too.

Completely true　　*Somewhat true/false*　　*Completely false*

　　　　Mostly true　　　　*Mostly false*

6 My mother/daughter and I often do small favors for one another, or give each other small gifts.

Completely true　　*Somewhat true/false*　　*Completely false*

　　　　Mostly true　　　　*Mostly false*

7 My mother/daughter is honest with me.

Completely true　　*Somewhat true/false*　　*Completely false*

　　　　Mostly true　　　　*Mostly false*

8 My mother/daughter would never purposely hurt my feelings.

Completely true   *Somewhat true/false*   *Completely false*

Mostly true   *Mostly false*

9 If we quarrel, we do not hold a grudge; after our emotions have cooled down, we can talk about the disagreement in a civil, adult manner.

Completely true   *Somewhat true/false*   *Completely false*

Mostly true   *Mostly false*

10 In difficult situations, such as illness or financial trouble, I know I can trust my mother/daughter to help me.

Completely true   *Somewhat true/false*   *Completely false*

Mostly true   *Mostly false*

SCORING ·····································

Each answer is awarded a specific number of points.

Completely true: *5 points*
Mostly true: *4 points*
Somewhat true/false: *3 points*
Mostly false: *2 points*
Completely false: *1 point*

50-40: Your mother/daughter relationship is loving, trusting and mature. Congratulations!
39-30: Could be better, but not bad at all.
Below 30: Do you really plan to rehash these issues for the rest of your life?

Are You Jealous of Your Siblings?

1 In school, my sibling got the best grades.

Completely true   Somewhat true/false   Completely false

Mostly true   Mostly false

2 I think I am the smartest of my siblings.

Completely true   Somewhat true/false   Completely false

Mostly true   Mostly false

3 My sibling is more athletic than the rest of the family.

Completely true   Somewhat true/false   Completely false

Mostly true   Mostly false

4 My sibling has always had more friends than me.

Completely true   Somewhat true/false   Completely false

Mostly true   Mostly false

5 I think I am more charismatic than my sibling.

Completely true   Somewhat true/false   Completely false

Mostly true   Mostly false

6 My sibling thinks he/she is the best looking person in our family.

Completely true   Somewhat true/false   Completely false

Mostly true   Mostly false

7 My career has been more successful than my siblings'.

Completely true   Somewhat true/false   Completely false

Mostly true   Mostly false

8 At birthdays, my siblings received more gifts than I did on my birthday.

Completely true   *Somewhat true/false*   *Completely false*

Mostly true   *Mostly false*

9 I was my mother's favorite.

Completely true   *Somewhat true/false*   *Completely false*

Mostly true   *Mostly false*

10 My sibling received more attention from our parents than I did.

Completely true   *Somewhat true/false*   *Completely false*

Mostly true   *Mostly false*

SCORING ··································

Each answer is awarded a specific number of points.

Completely true: *5 points*
Mostly true: *4 points*
Somewhat true/false: *3 points*
Mostly false: *2 points*
Completely false: *1 point*

50-40: You are seething with resentment.
39-30: You've got a touch of sibling rivalry, but it's not out of control.
Below 30: You and your siblings are pals.